Drayton Ontario and Area in Colour Photos, Saving Our History One Photo at a Time

Photography
by Barbara Raué
2014

Series Name:
Cruising Ontario

Book 80: Drayton and Area

Cover photo: 19 Edward Street, Drayton

Series Name: Cruising Ontario
Saving Our History One Photo at a Time

Other Books by Barbara Raue

Coins of Gold

Arrows, Indians and Love

The Life and Times of Barbara
Volume 1: Inventions That Have Enhanced My Life
Volume 2: Entertainment That I Have Enjoyed
Volume 3: East Coast Trips
Volume 4: Olympics Have Always Intrigued Me
Volume 5: Wonders of the World
Volume 6: Caribbean Cruises We Have Enjoyed
Volume 7: Animals
Volume 8: Storms and Other Major Disasters in My Lifetime
Volume 9: Wars, Terrorist Attacks and Major Disasters

The Cromwell Family Book

Laura Secord Discovered

Visit Barbara's website to view all of her books
http://barbararaue.ca

Centre Wellington is a township in south-central Ontario. The primary communities in the township are Elora and Fergus. Some of the smaller communities are **Alma, Salem, and Speedside.**

Parker was a settlement in Ontario, located along the Elora-Saugeen road. Settlers moved to the area to begin new lives and to farm. To provide accommodation for travelers in horse-drawn vehicles, a hotel opened in 1850. In 1865, Thomas Burns opened a post office which brought a few neighbouring businesses to the area. As travel became more modern, the need for overnight stay diminished and the town began to dwindle. It is still used for farming today but the hotel and post office have closed. The school house is still standing and is a private home, painted pink.

Conestogo Lake Conservation Area is in the heart of Mennonite country. It is on a y-shaped lake that stretches six kilometres up each arm. A unique feature of this area is the huge concrete flood control dam and reservoir surrounded by large tracts of forest, giving the appearance that the park is in northern Ontario. This is a multi-recreational use park for camping, power boating, sailing, water skiing, canoeing and fishing.

Glen Allan is located in Wellington County southeast of Conestogo Lake.

Yatton is located in Wellington County. The area was settled by people in the early 1820s, when Black Loyalists, African-Canadians and African-American immigrants arrived in the wilderness of the Queen's Bush. Until the late 1840s the Queen's Bush remained an unorganized territory. Three African-Canadian churches were constructed in the Queen's Bush and one of them was in Yatton which Reverend Samuel H. Brown established on his farm.

Drayton is a community in Wellington County. The village is on the corner of Wellington Road 8 and Wellington Road 11, and is located northwest of Fergus and southwest of Arthur.

Table of Contents

Alma

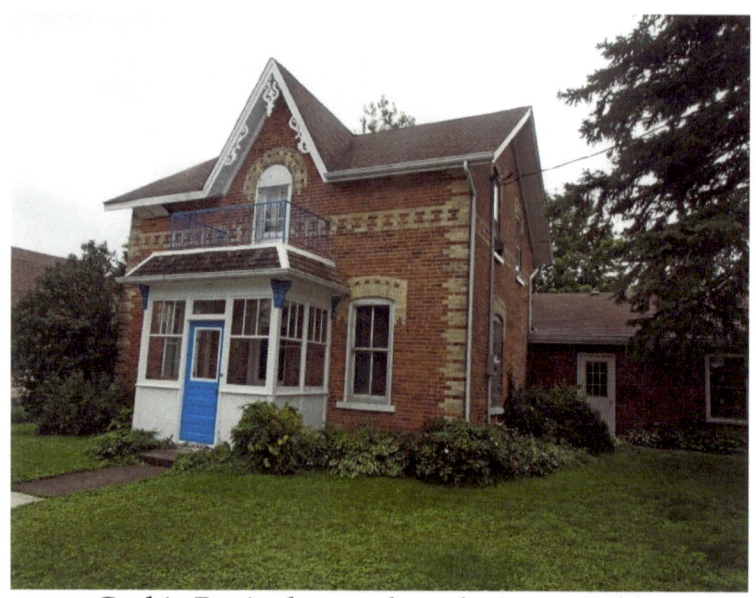

Gothic Revival, vergeboard trim on gable,
dichromatic brickwork

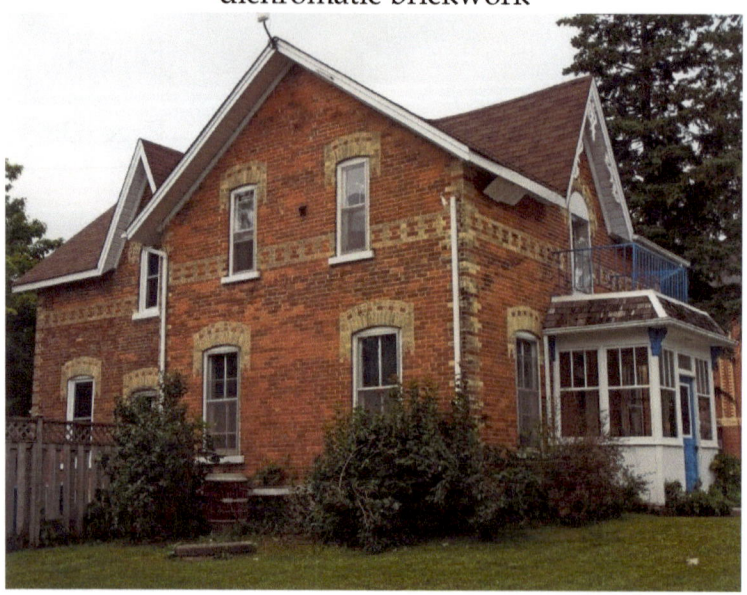

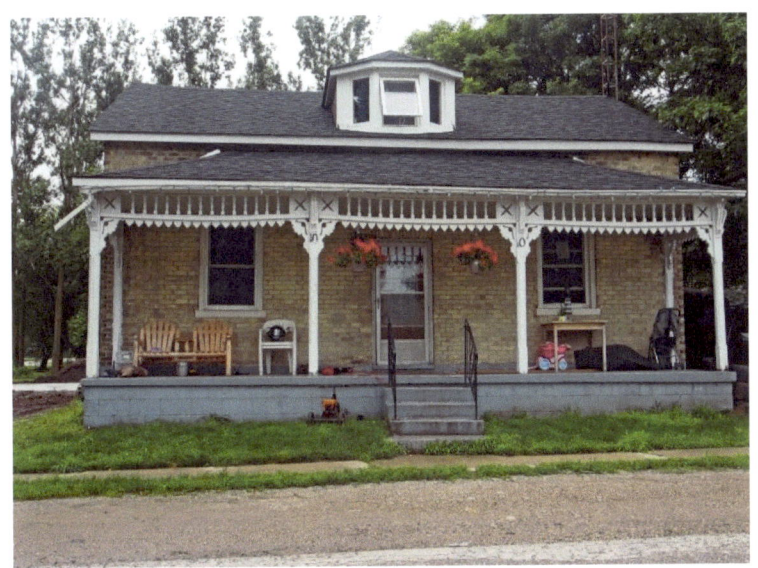

Yellow brick, dormer in attic

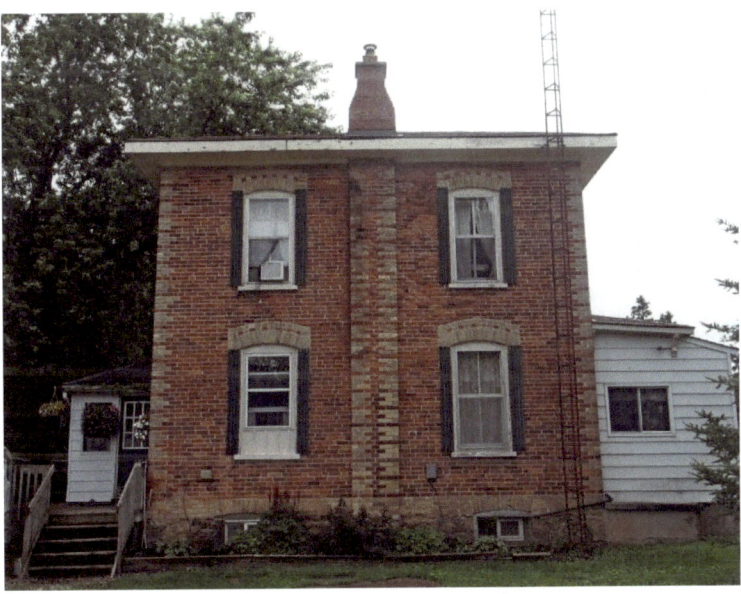

Italianate, corner quoins

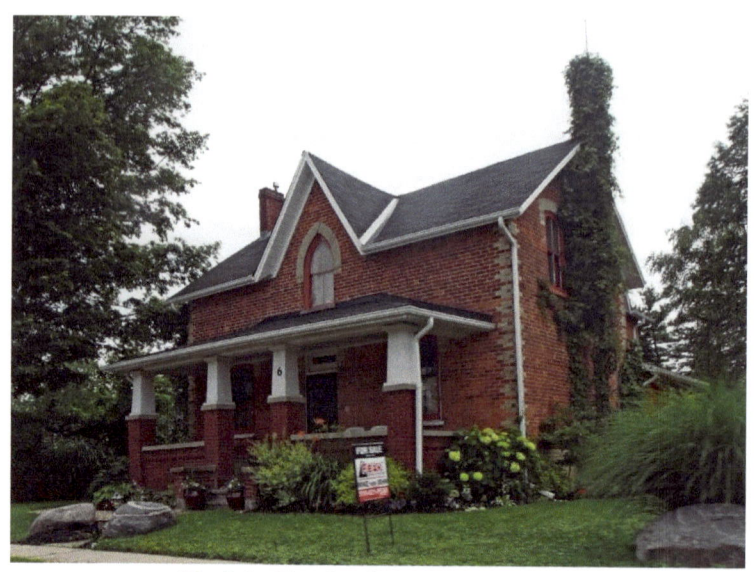

Gothic Revival, corner quoins

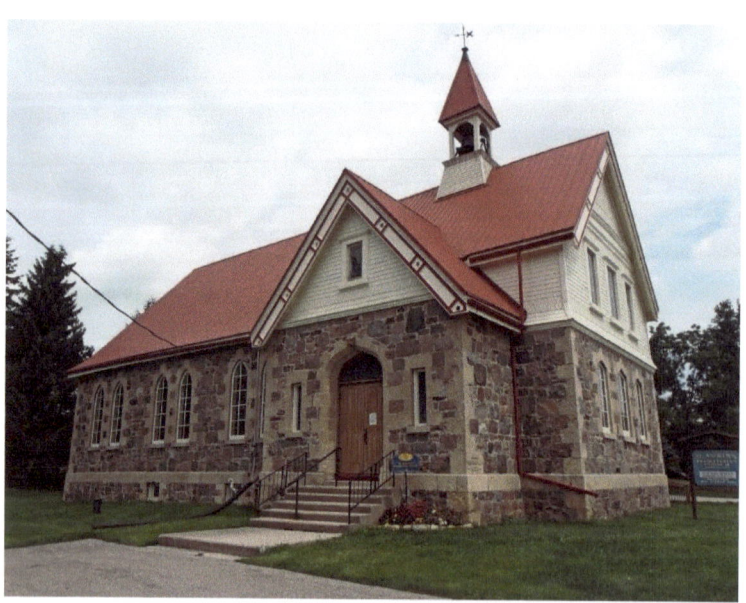

Cobblestone architecture

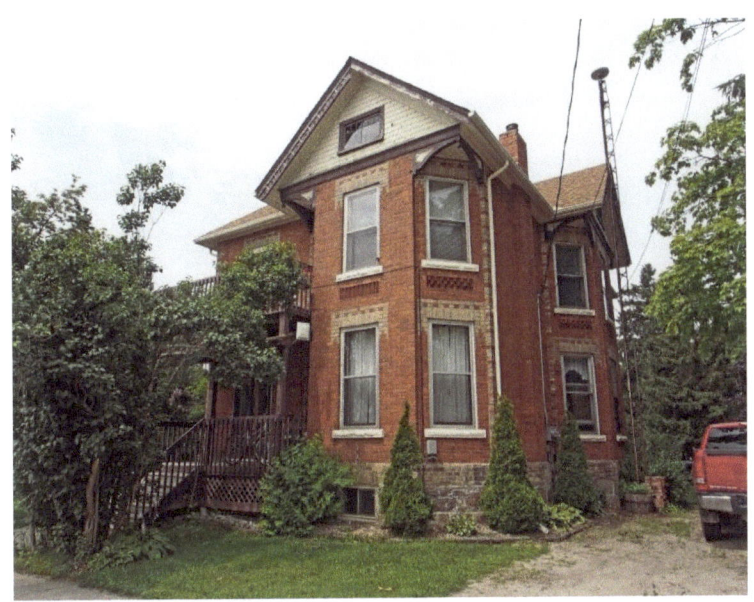

Dichromatic brickwork

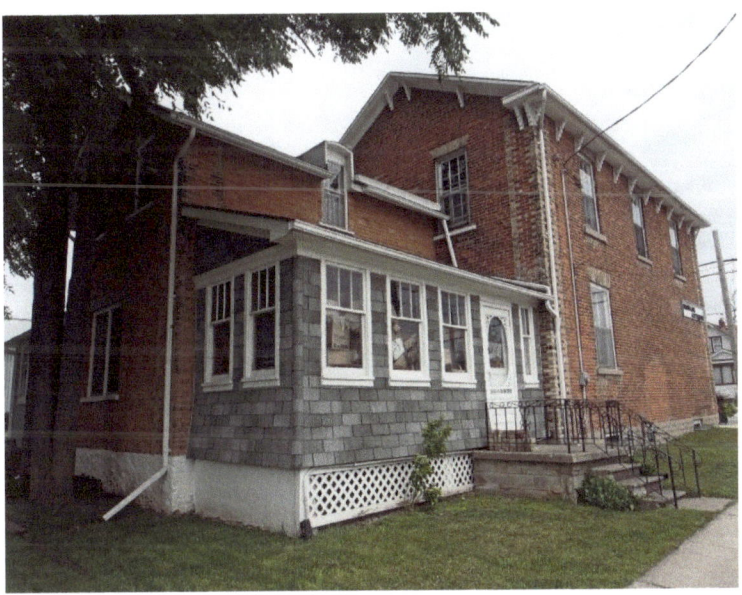

Cornice brackets

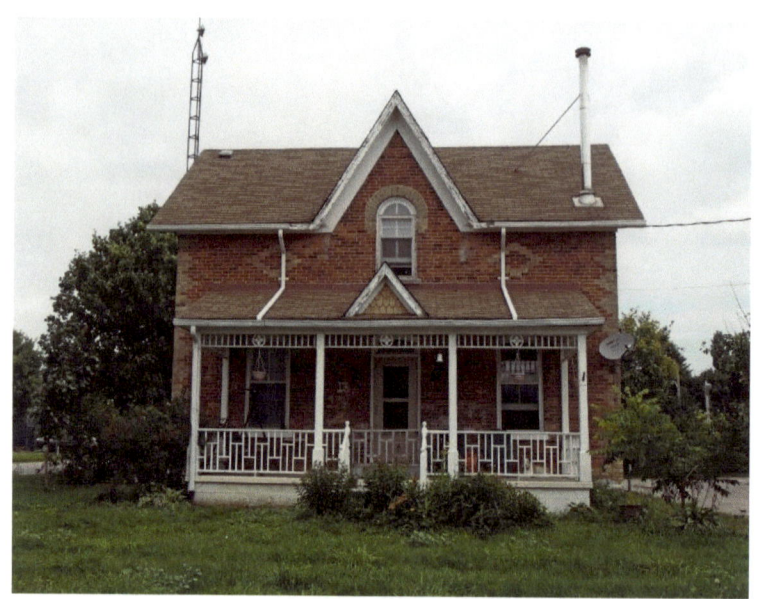

Gothic Revival

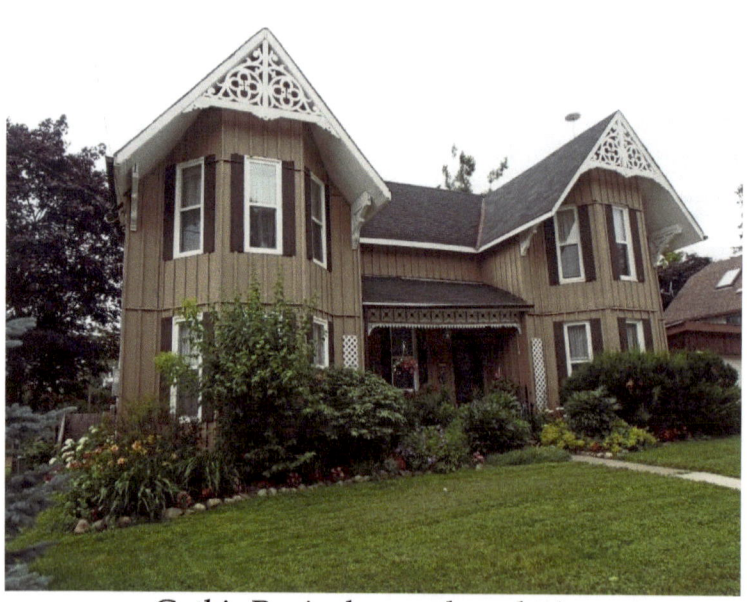

Gothic Revival, vergeboard trim

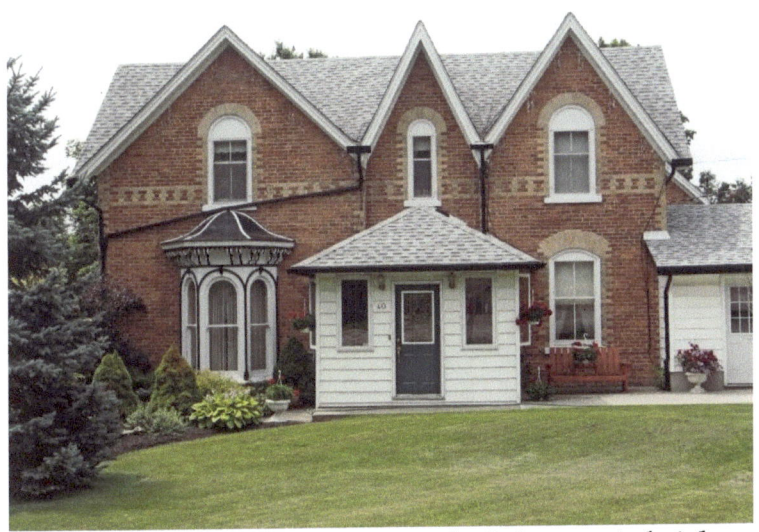

Triple gable Gothic Revival, dichromatic brickwork,
bay window, arched window voussoirs

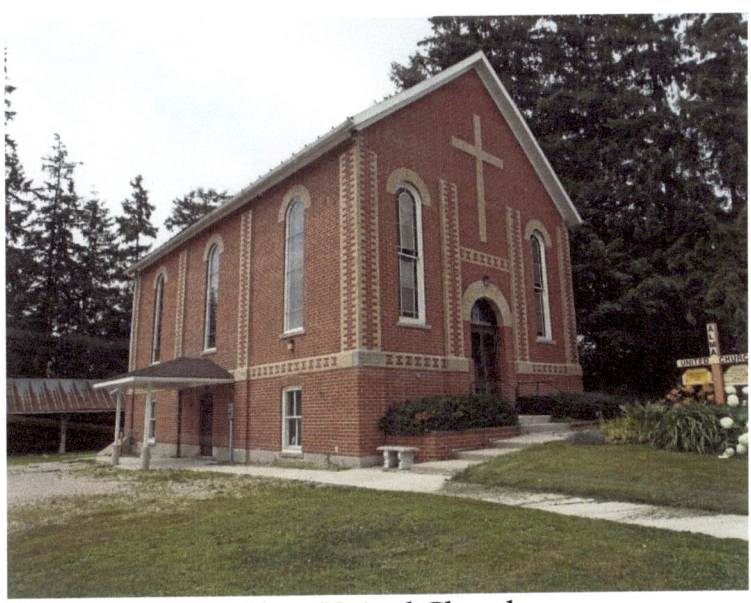

Alma United Church
Dichromatic brickwork

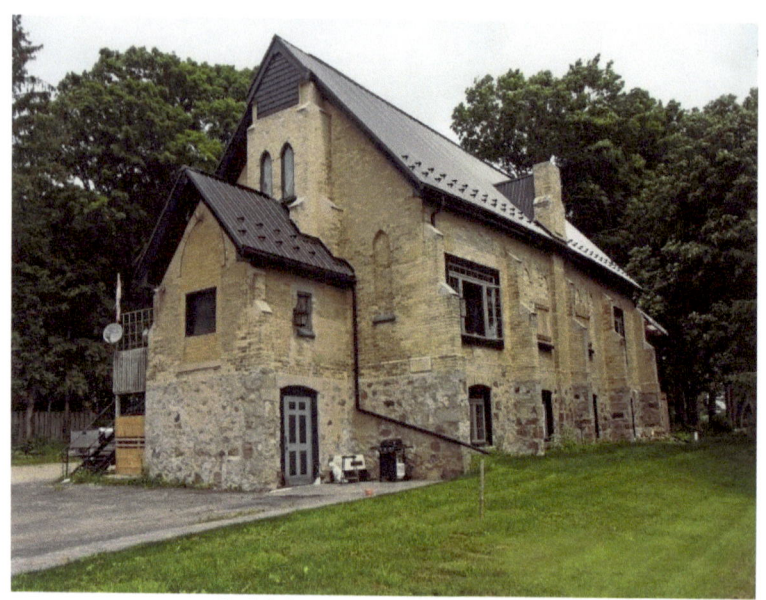

Cobblestone architecture

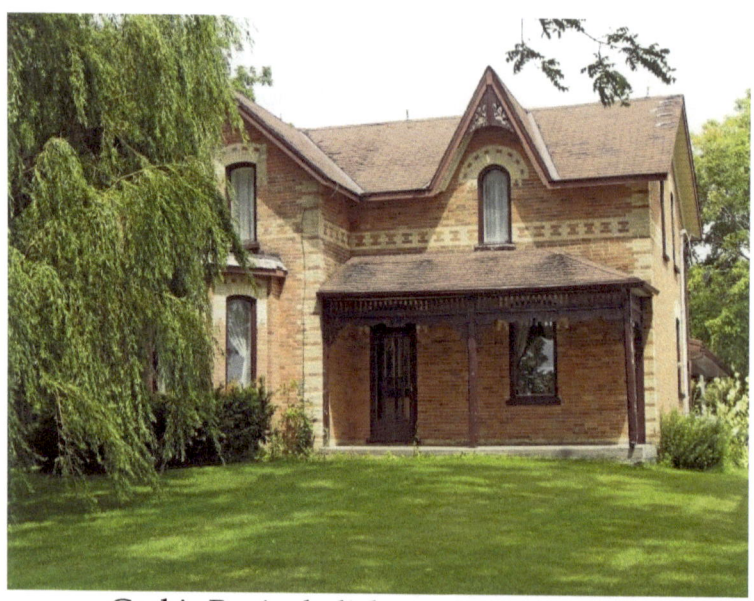

Gothic Revival, dichromatic brickwork

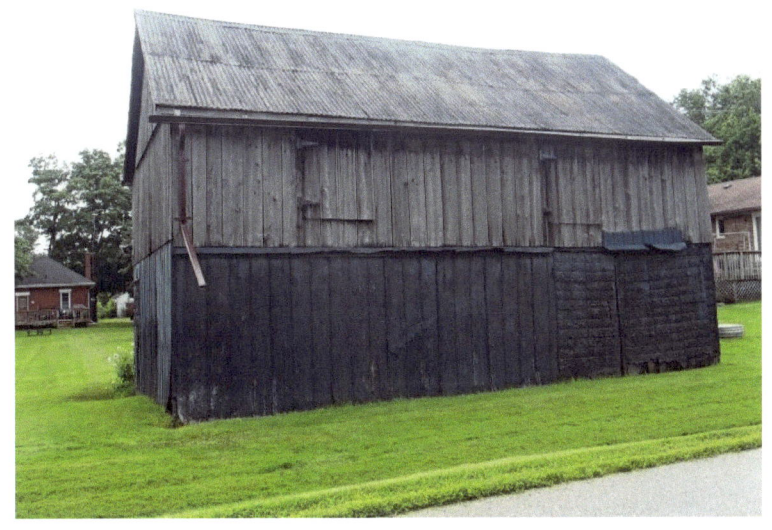

Parker

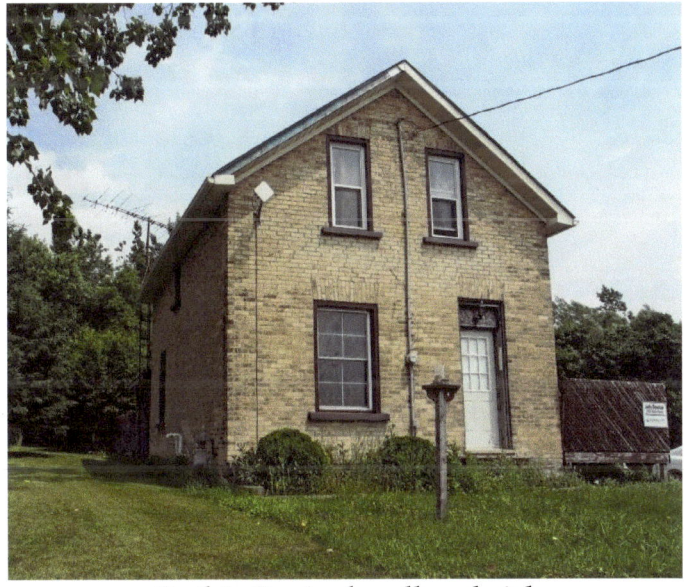

Gothic Revival, yellow brick

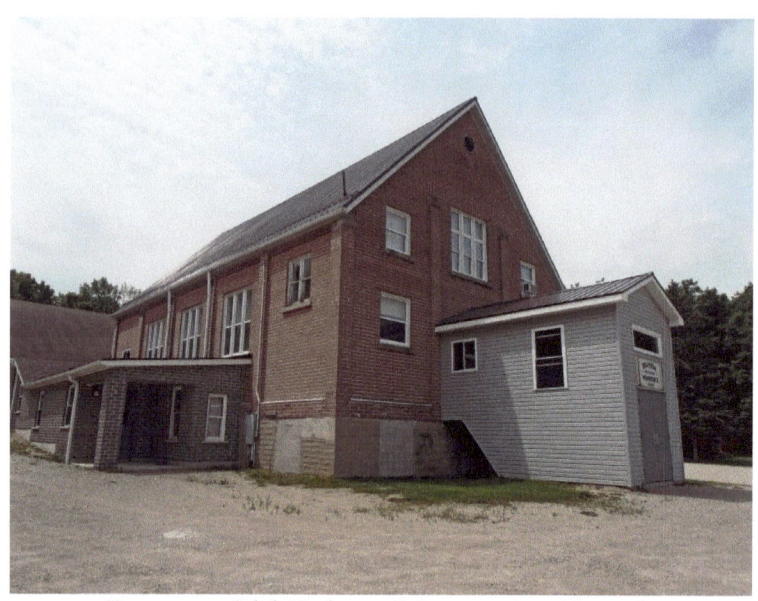

Drayton Old Colony Mennonite Church

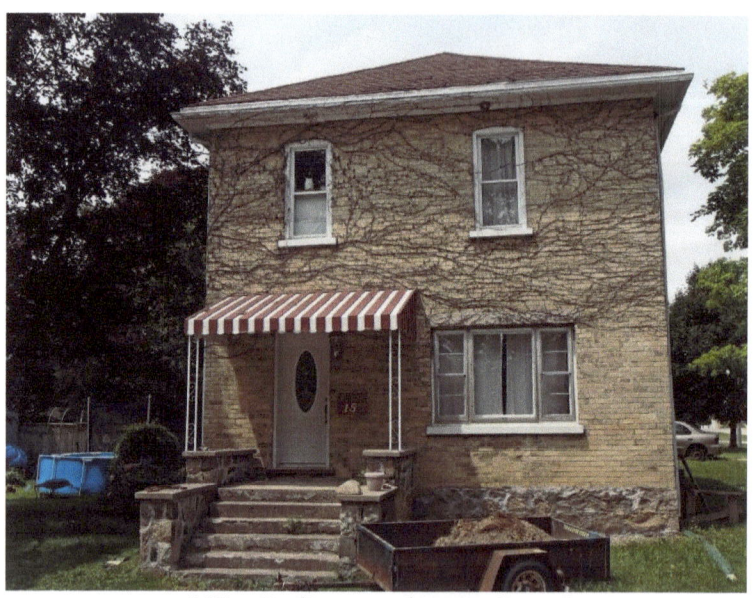

#15 – Italianate, hipped roof

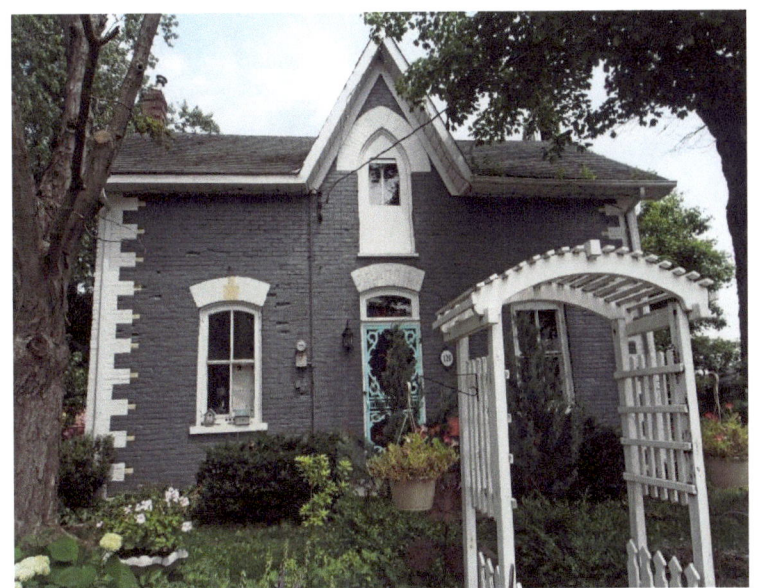

#120 – Gothic Revival, corner quoins

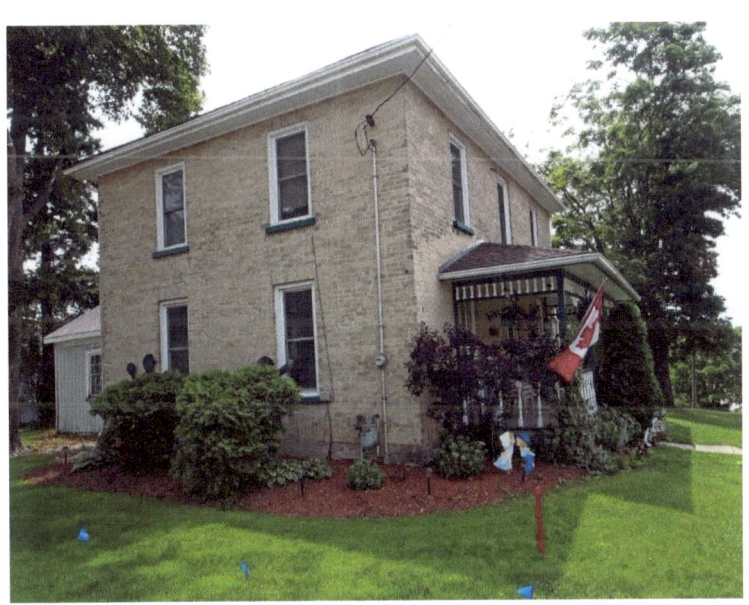

Italianate style

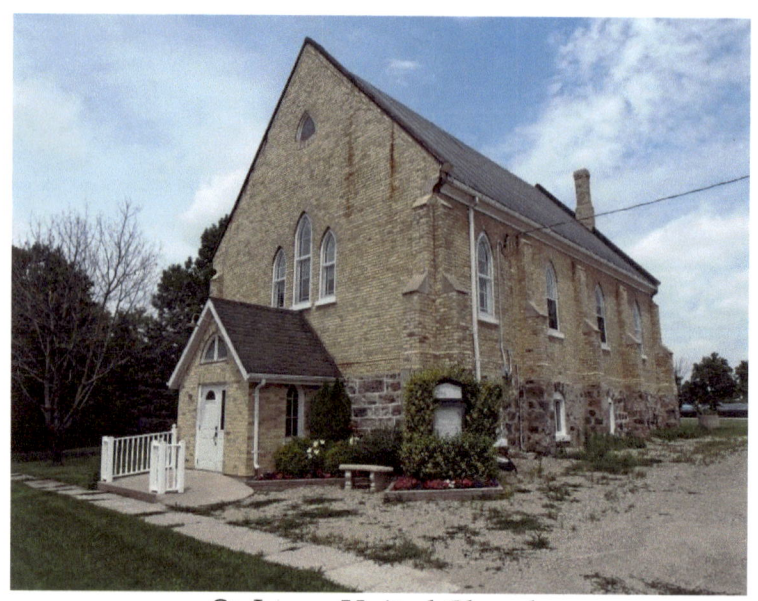

St. James United Church
Gothic Revival, lancet windows, cobblestone

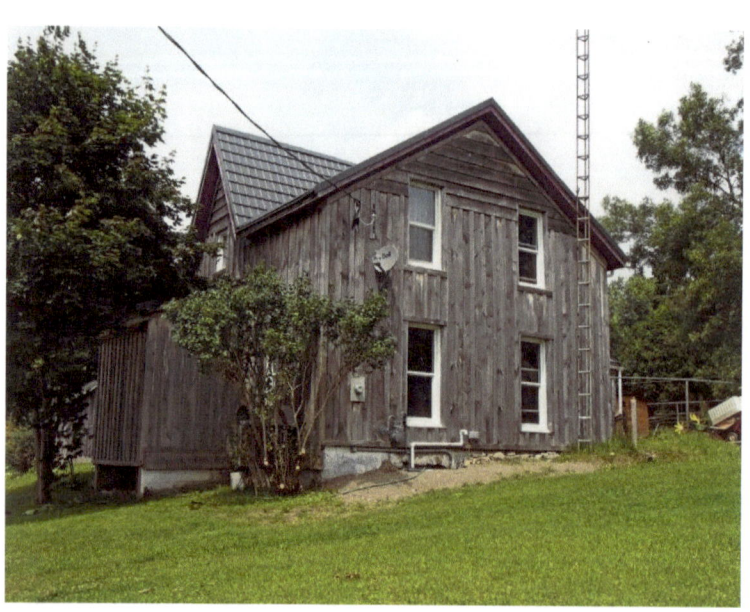

Conestogo Dam and Reservoir completed in 1958

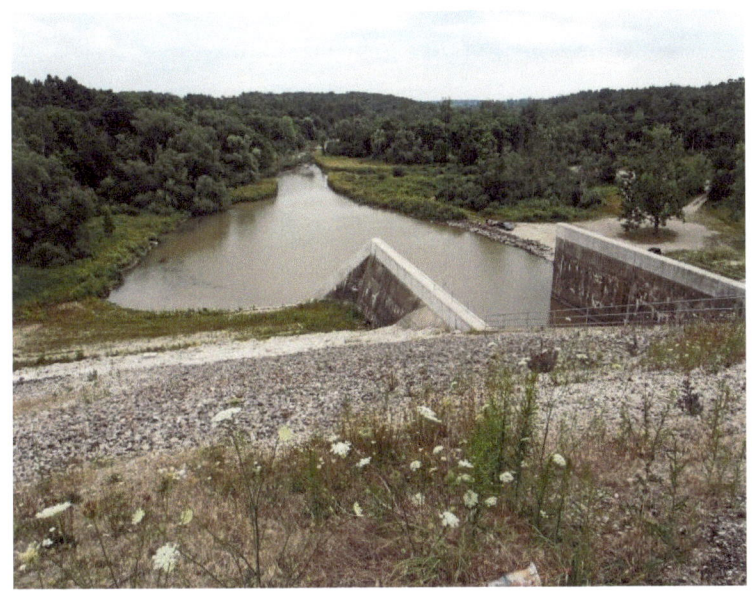

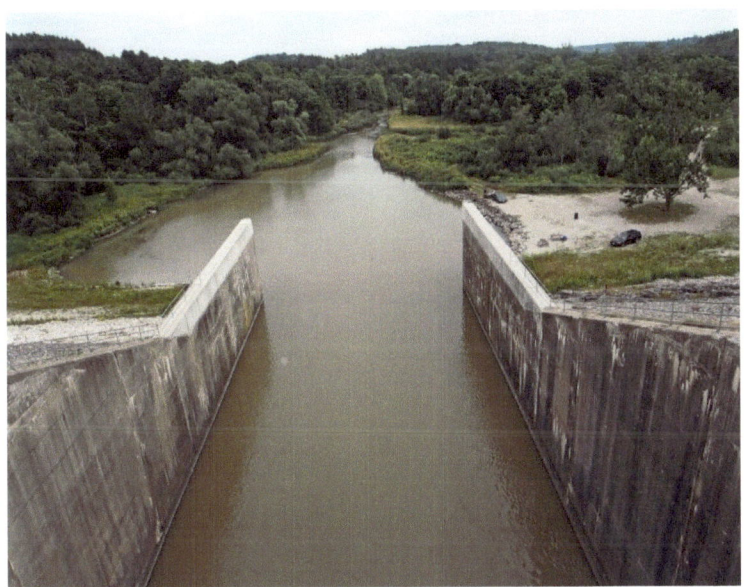

Conestogo Lake

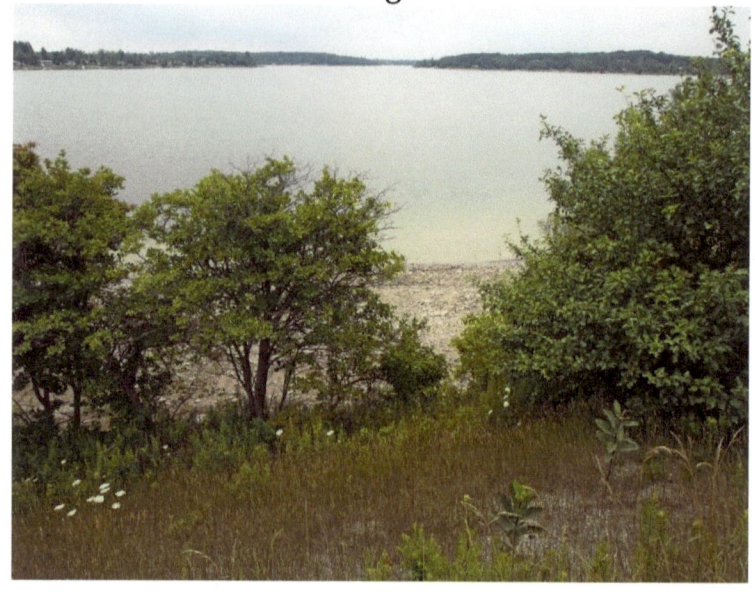

Glen Allan

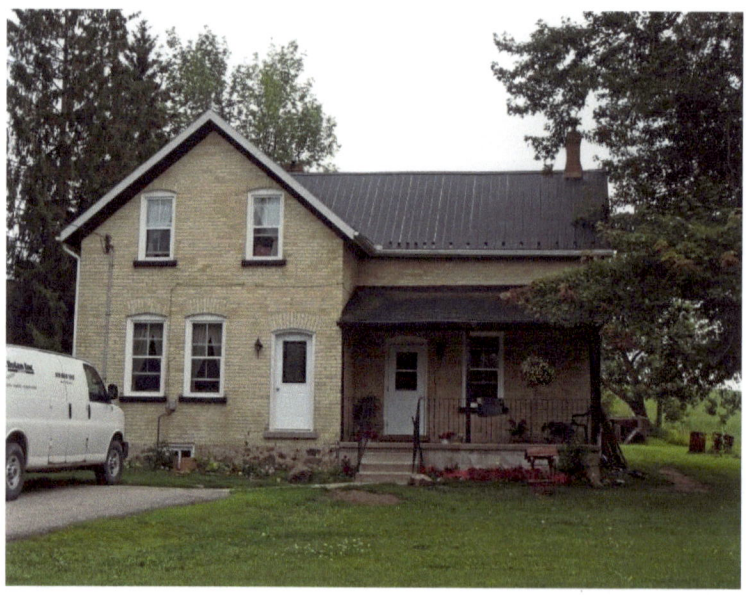

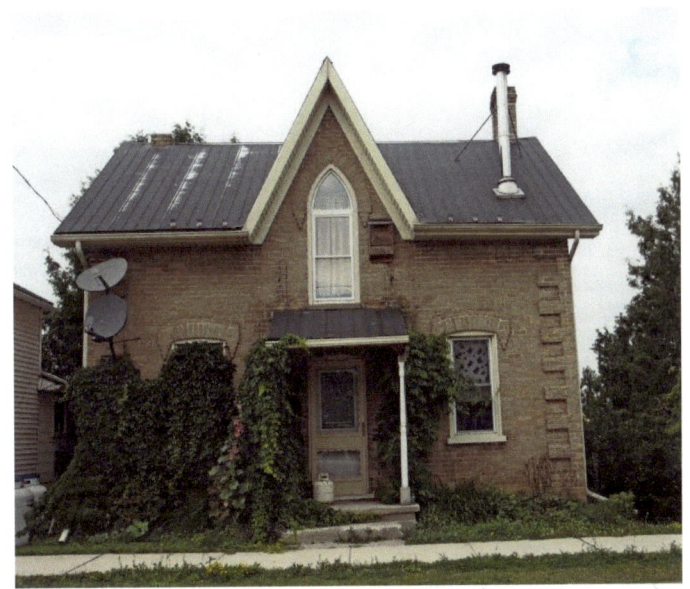

Gothic Revival – corner quoins

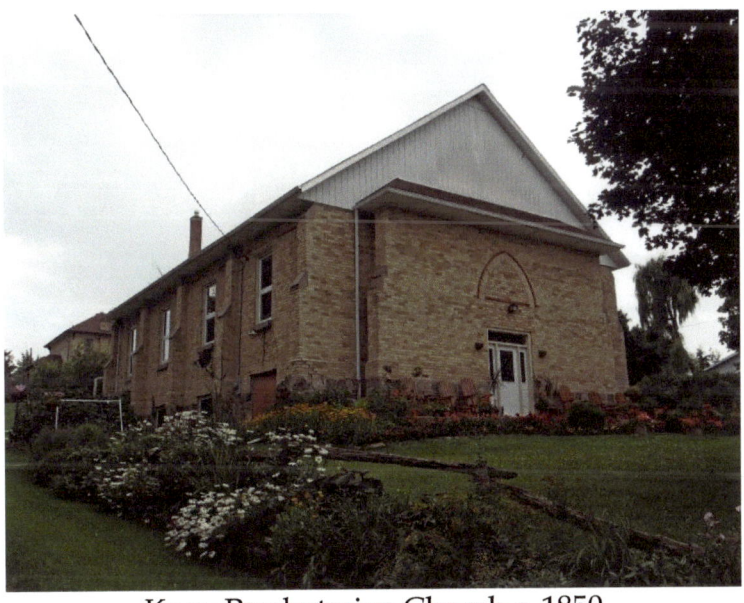

Knox Presbyterian Church c. 1850

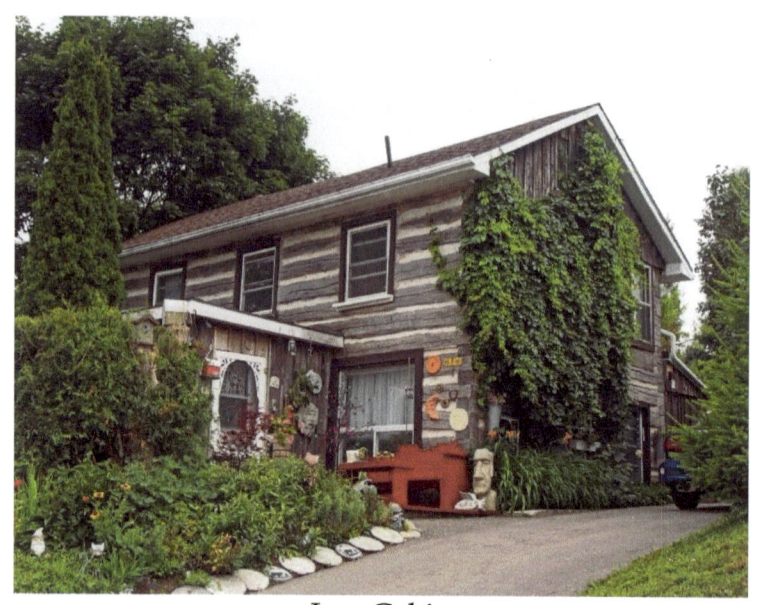

Log Cabin

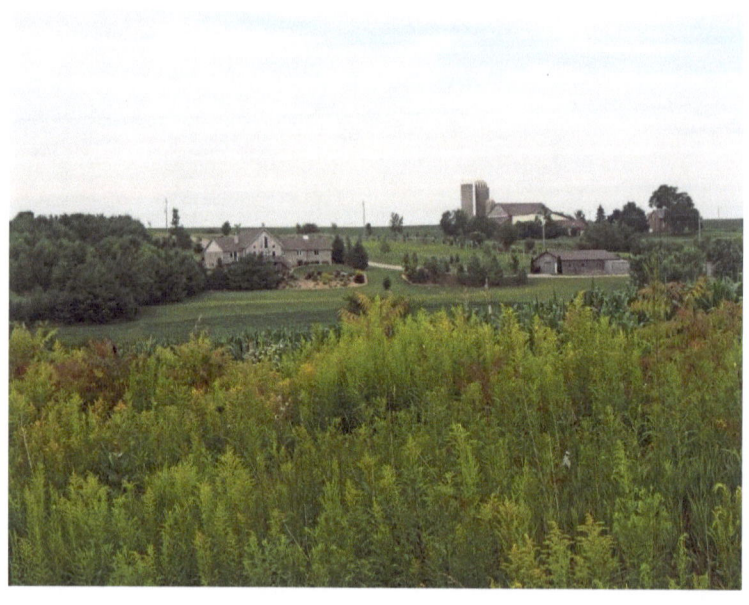

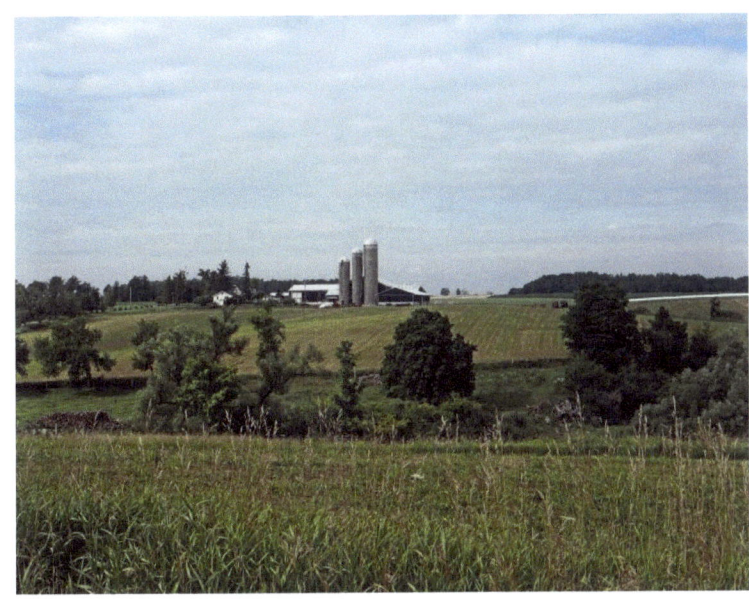

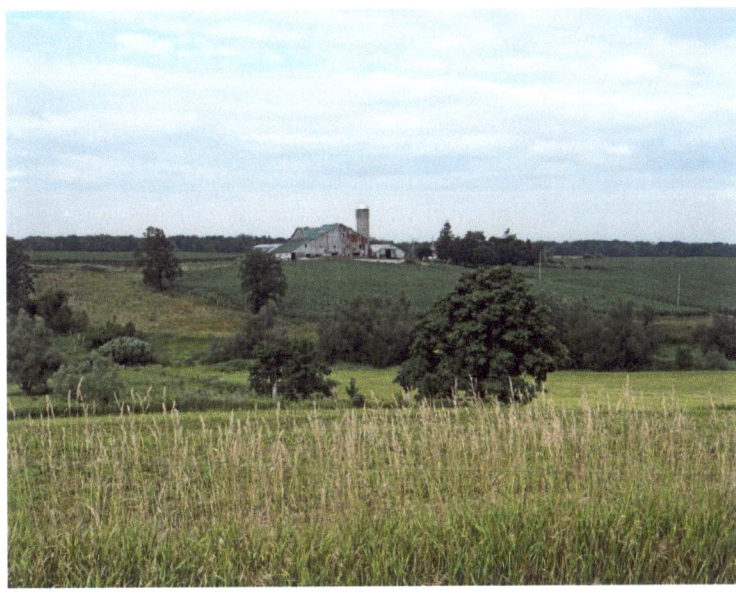

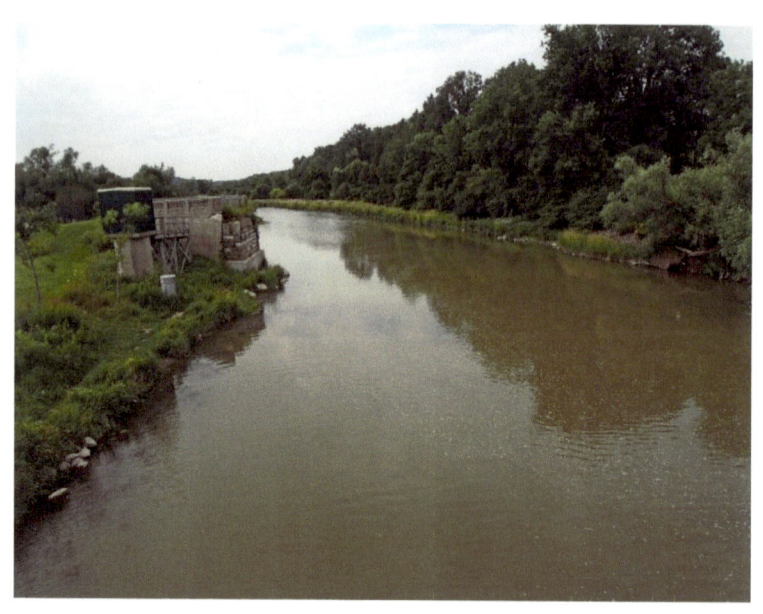

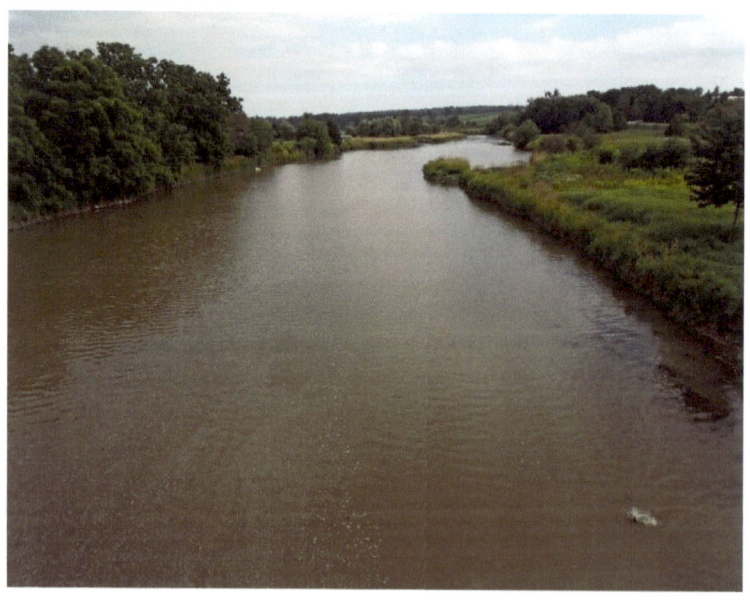

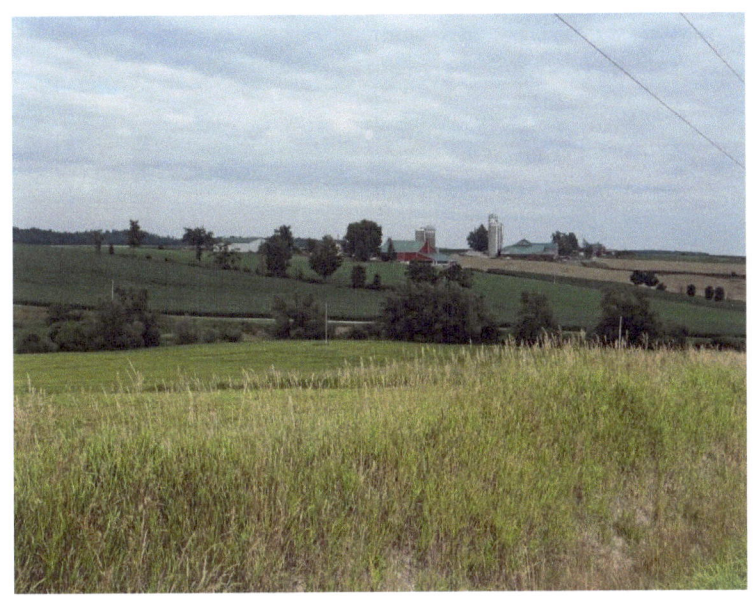

Yatton

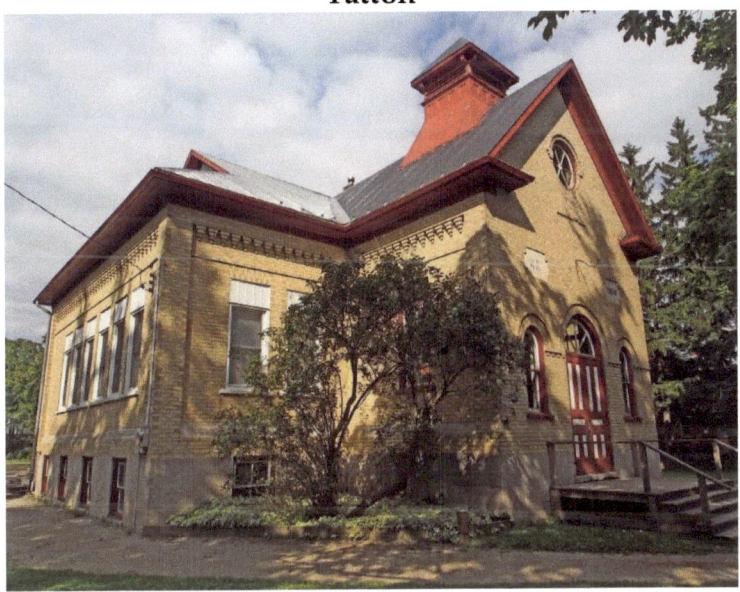

S.S. No. 1 Peel School -1926

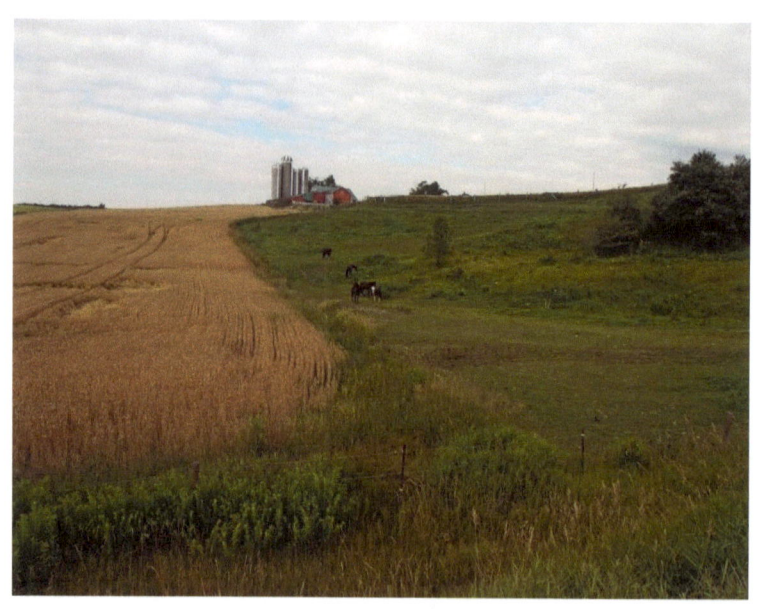

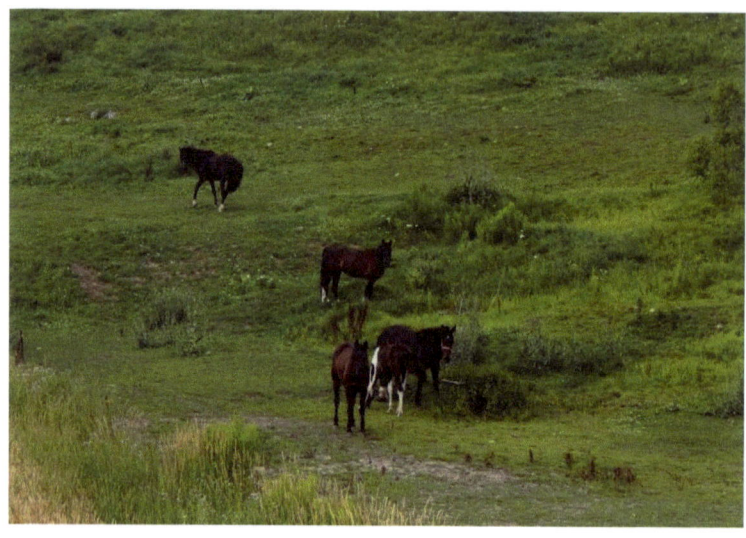

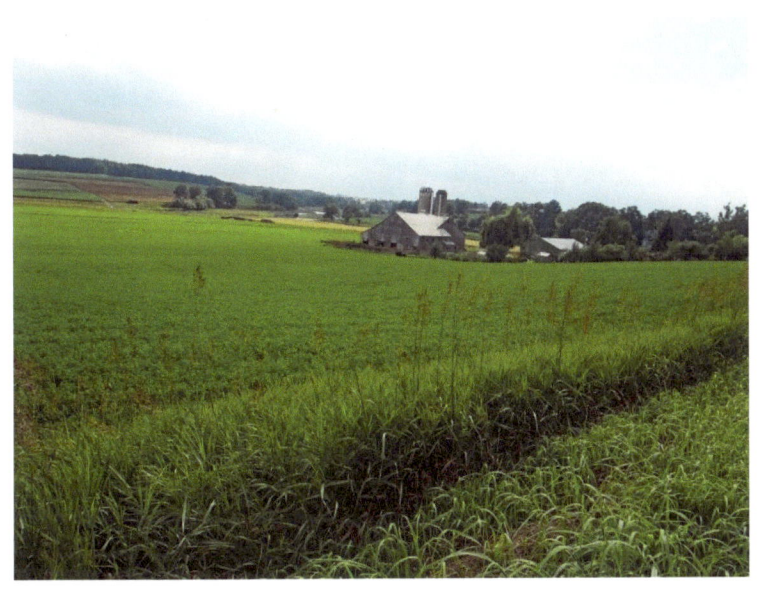

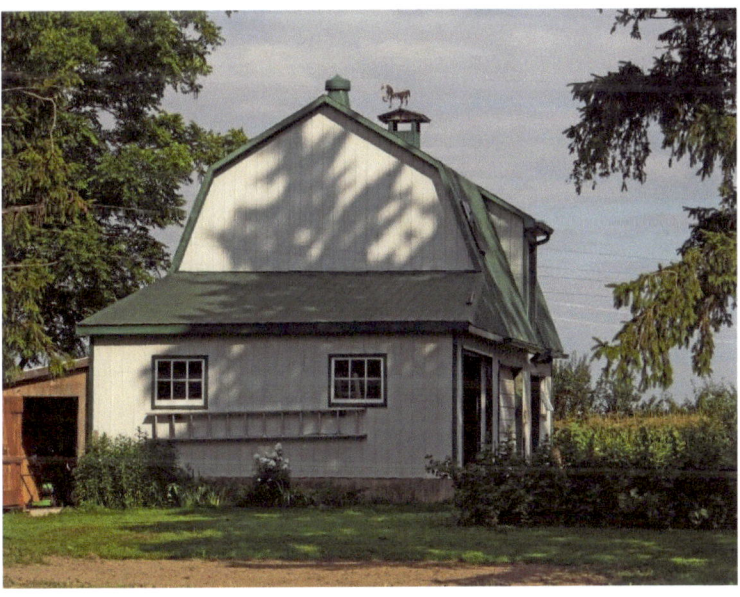

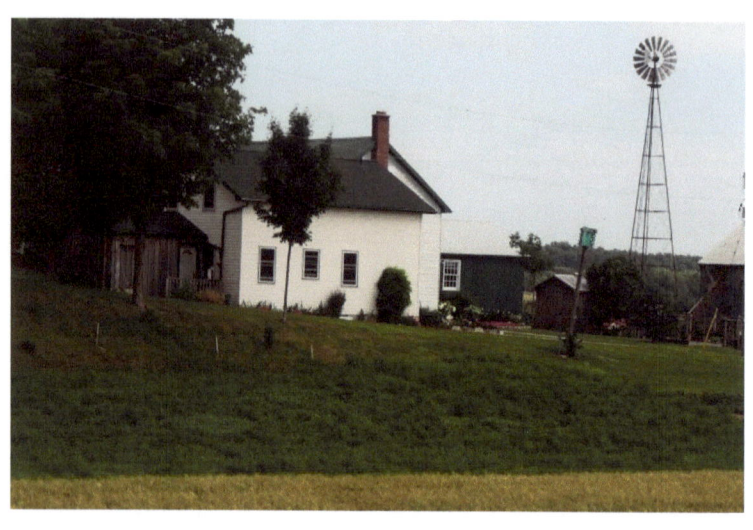

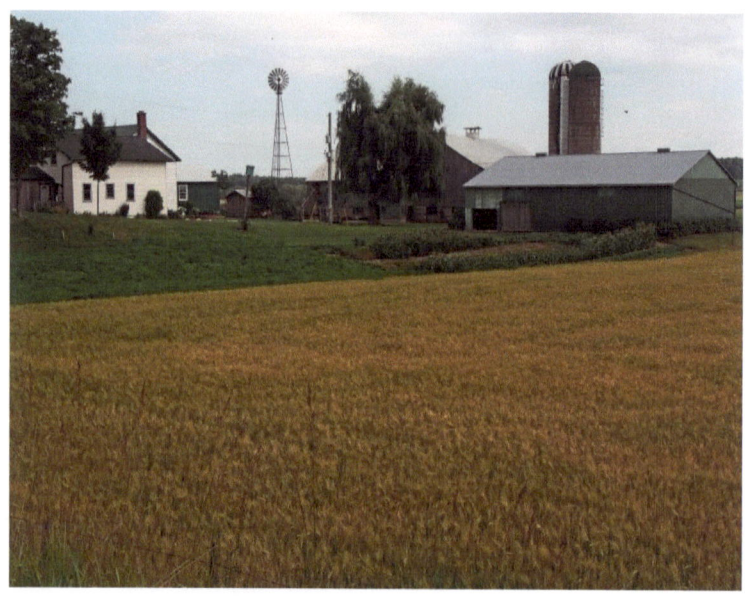

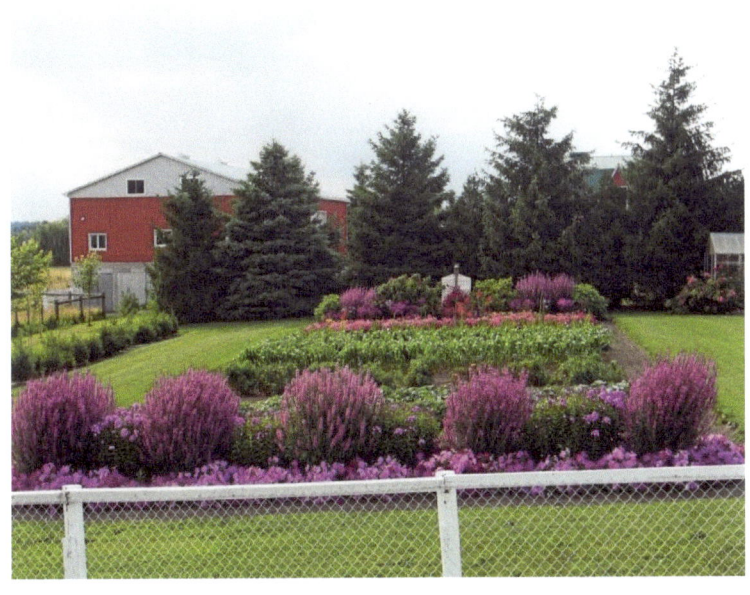

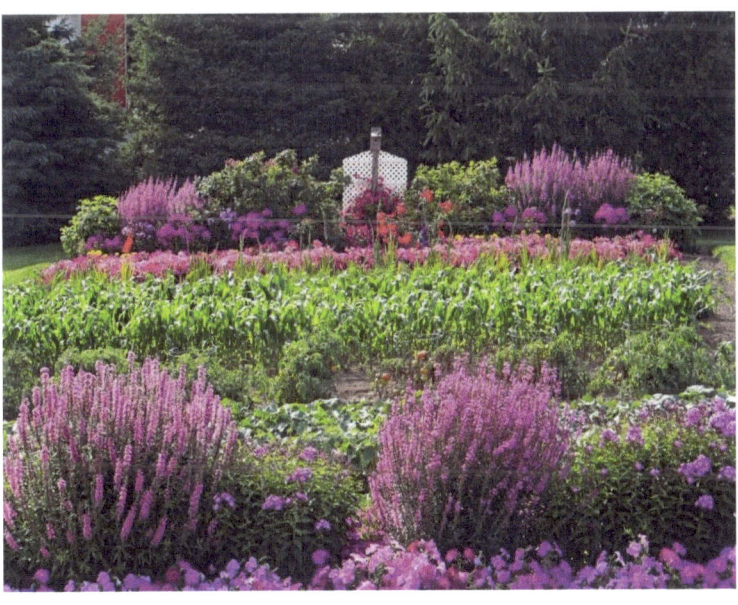

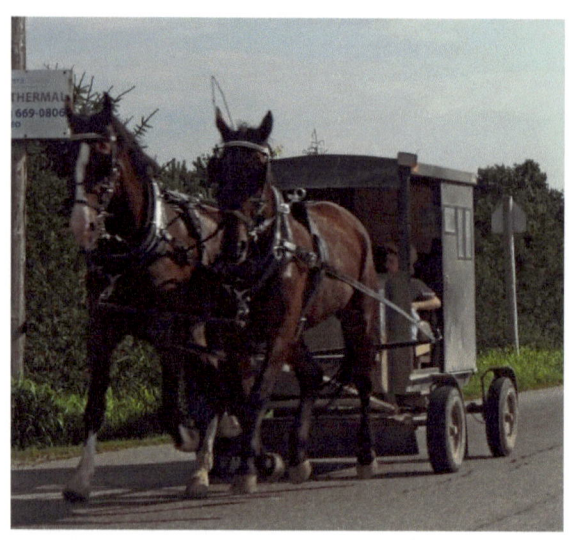

Drayton

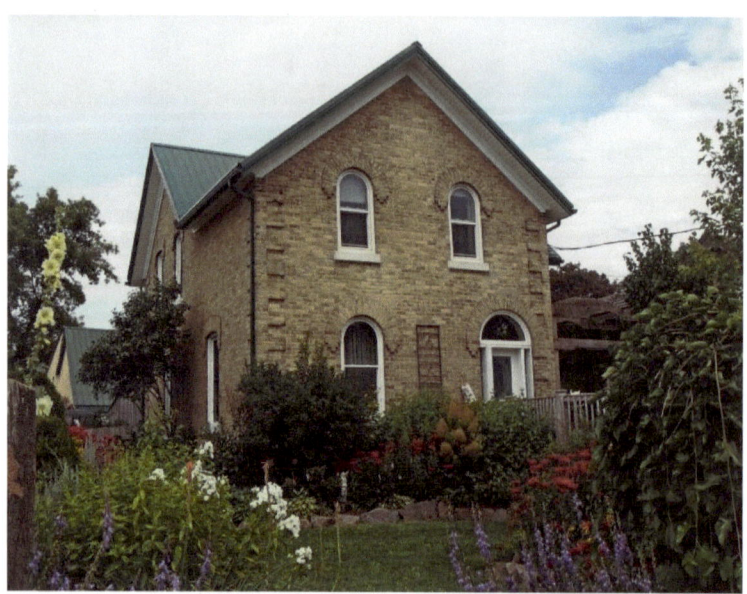

Gothic Revival, corner quoins

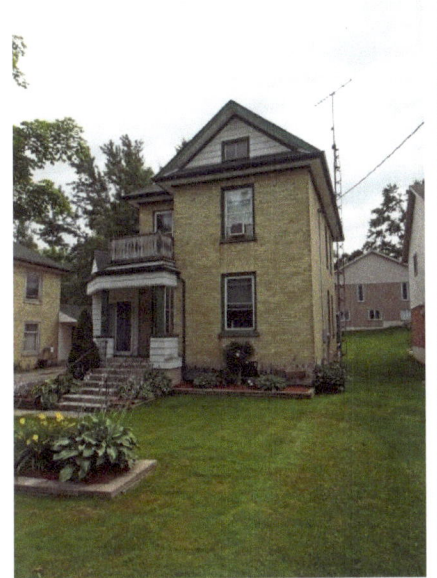

27 Main Street
Edwardian

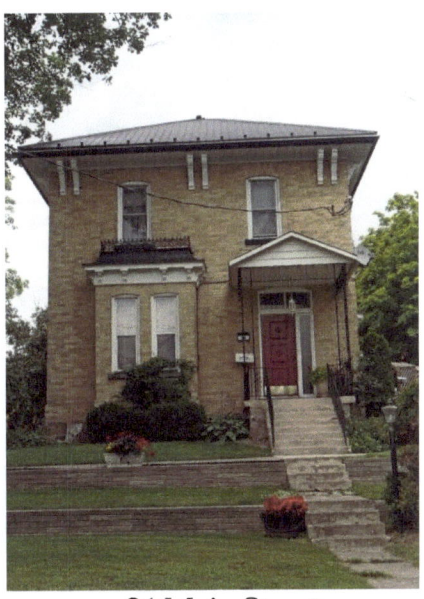

24 Main Street
Italianate, cornice brackets

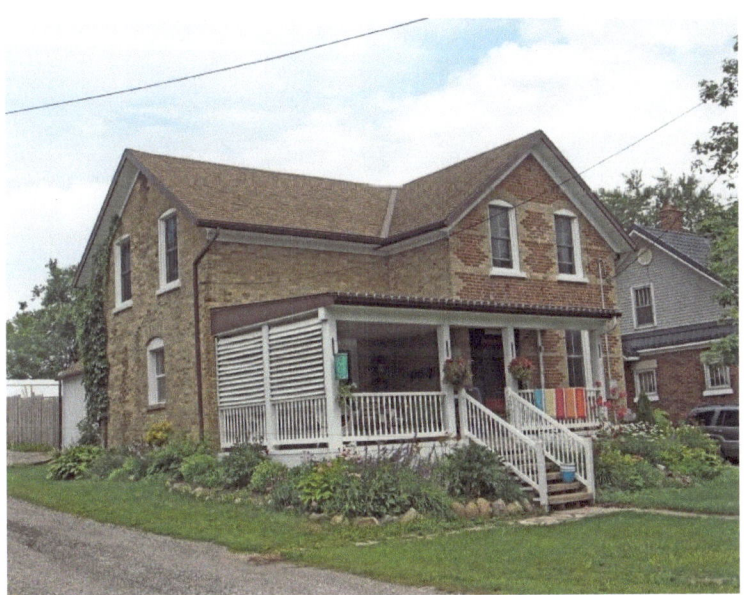

36 Main Street – dichromatic brickwork

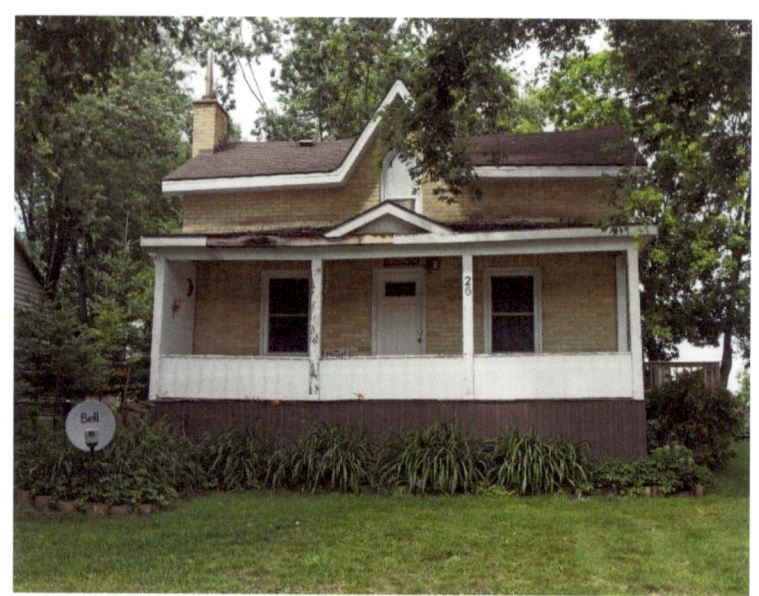

26 Main Street – Gothic Revival

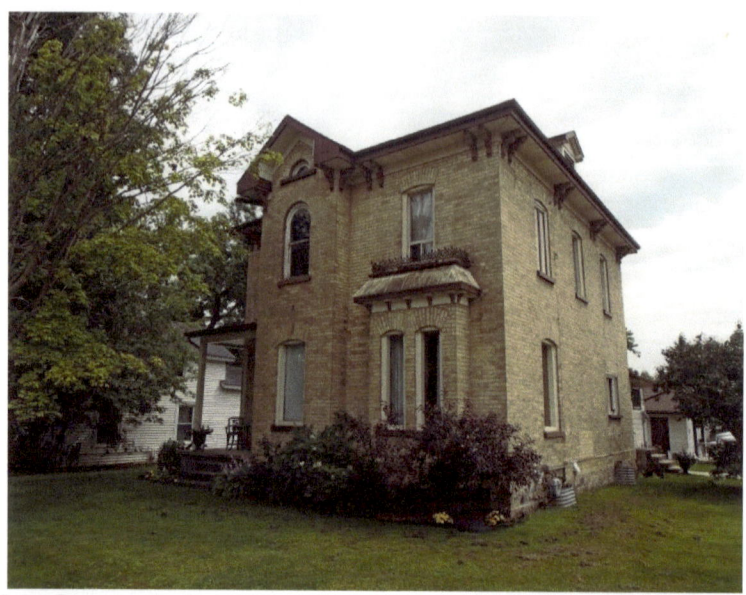

Main Street – Italianate with two-and-a-half storey frontispiece, cornice brackets, bay window with iron cresting above

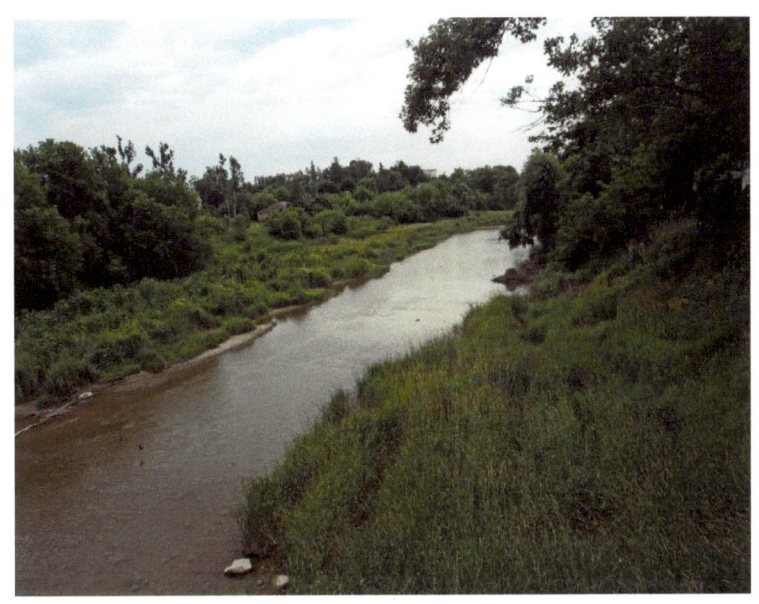

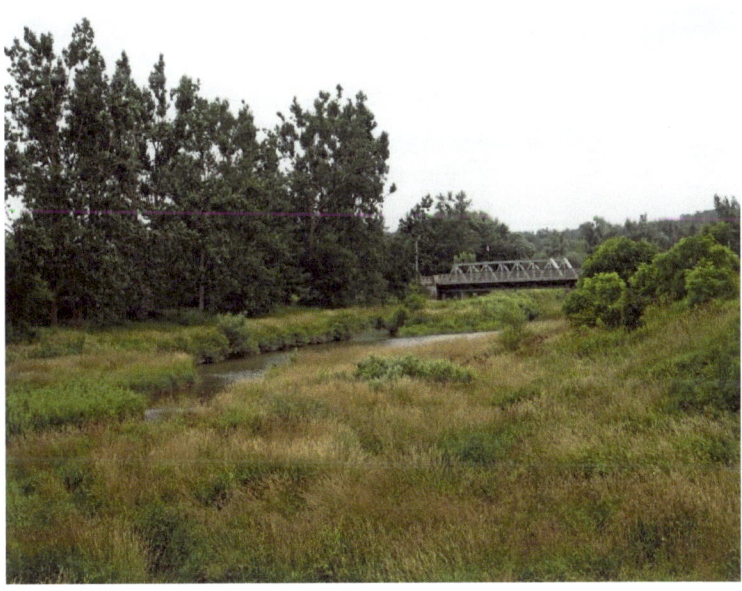

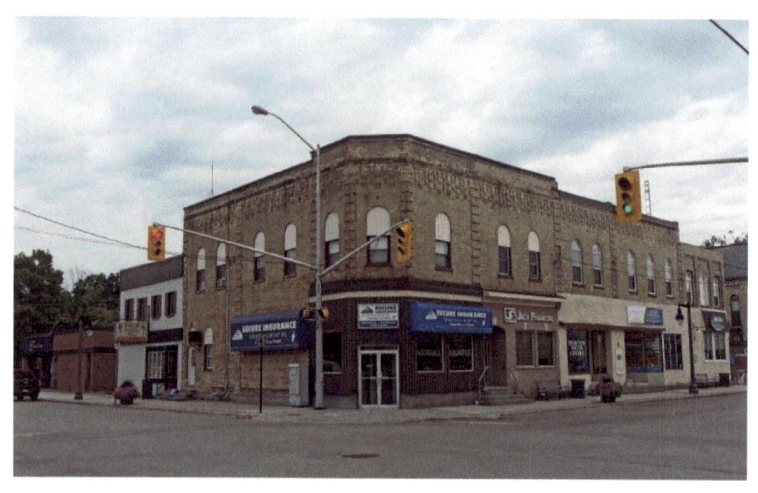

Downtown Drayton

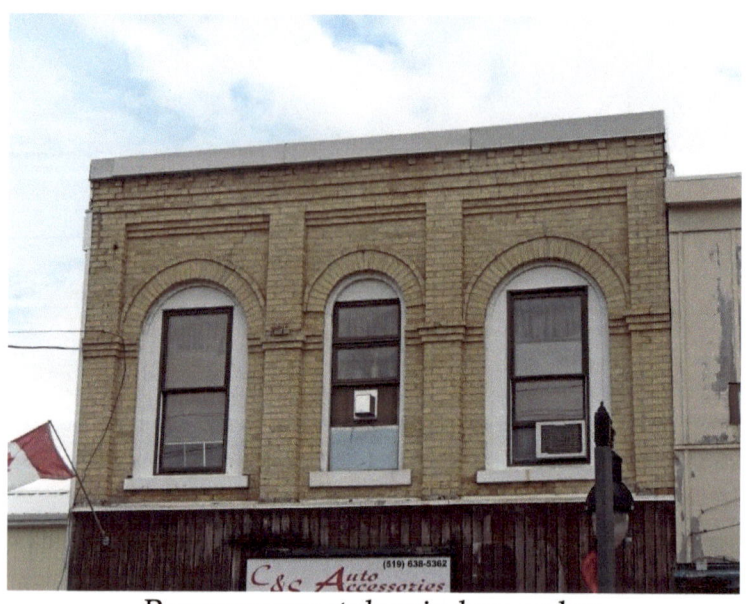

Romanesque style window arches

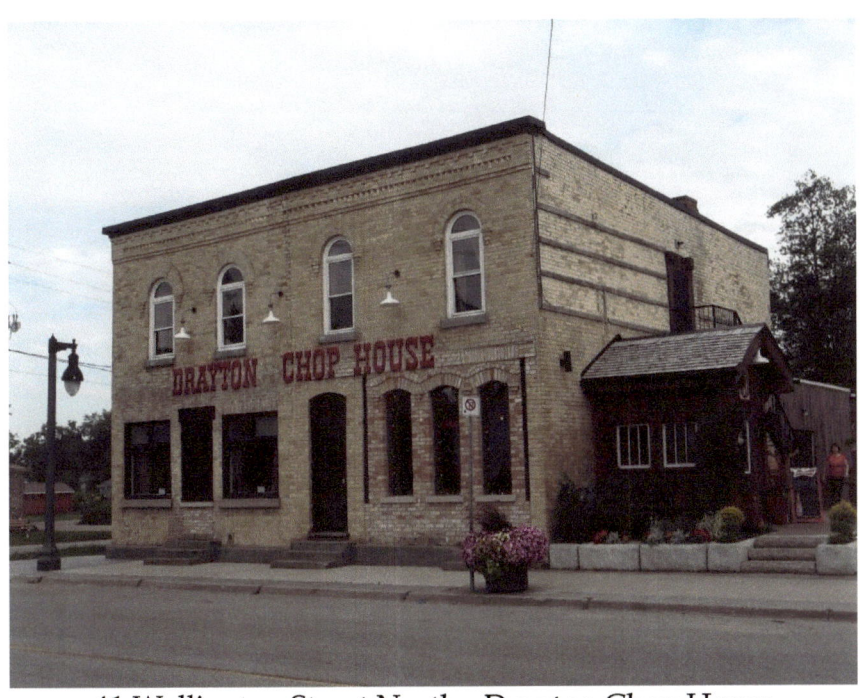

41 Wellington Street North - Drayton Chop House

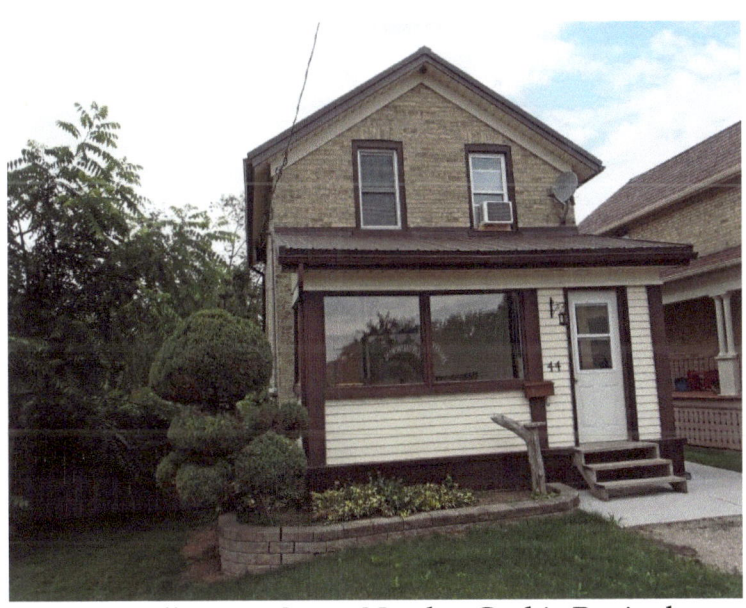

44 Wellington Street North – Gothic Revival

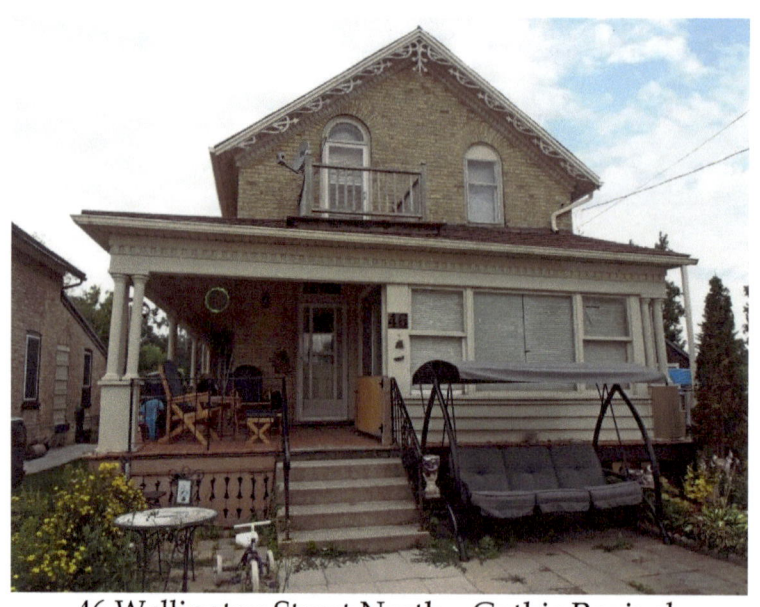

46 Wellington Street North – Gothic Revival,
vergeboard trim and finial on gable

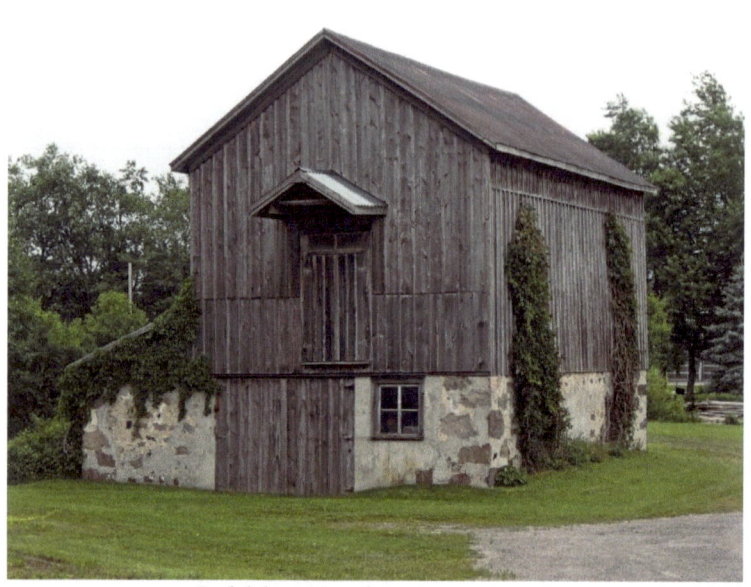

Cobblestone basement wall

Views from the Emerson Simmons Bridge (built 1957)

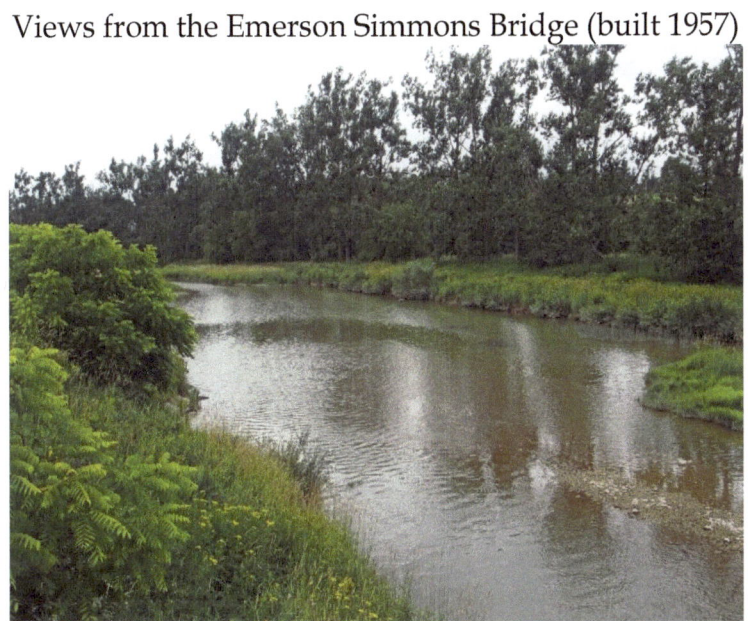

Great Blue Heron fishing

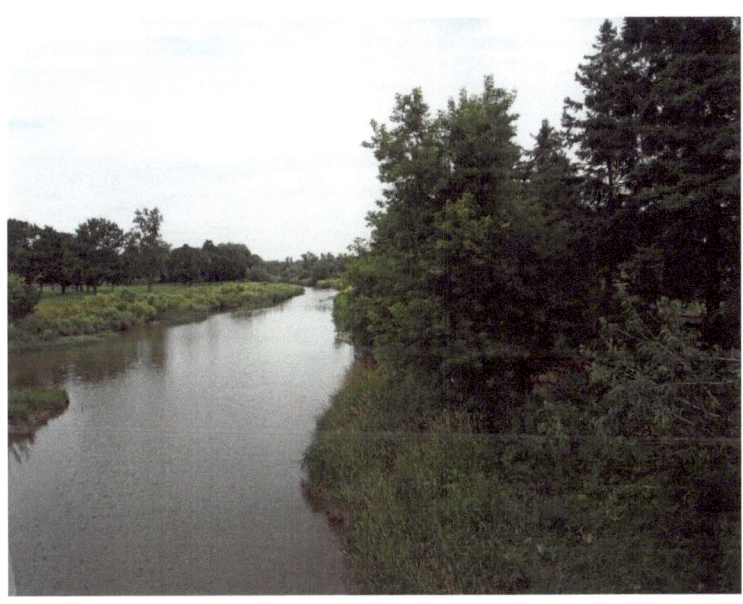

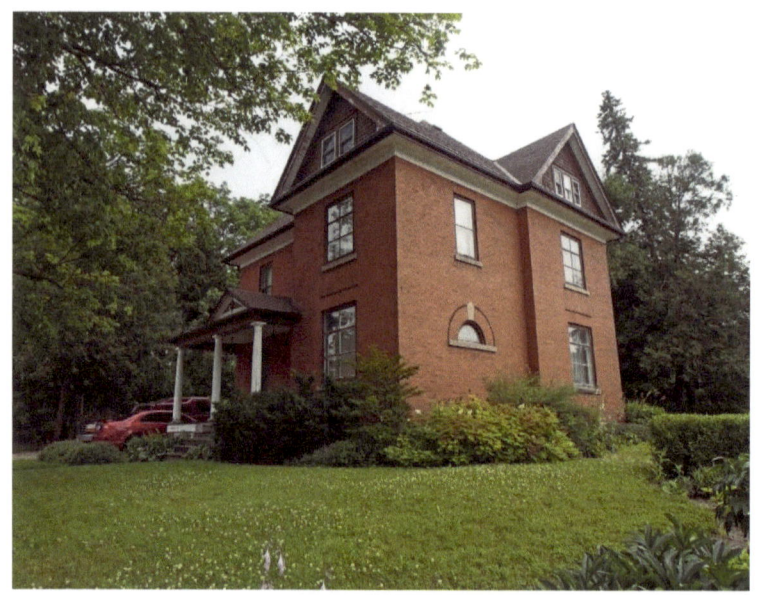

9 High Street

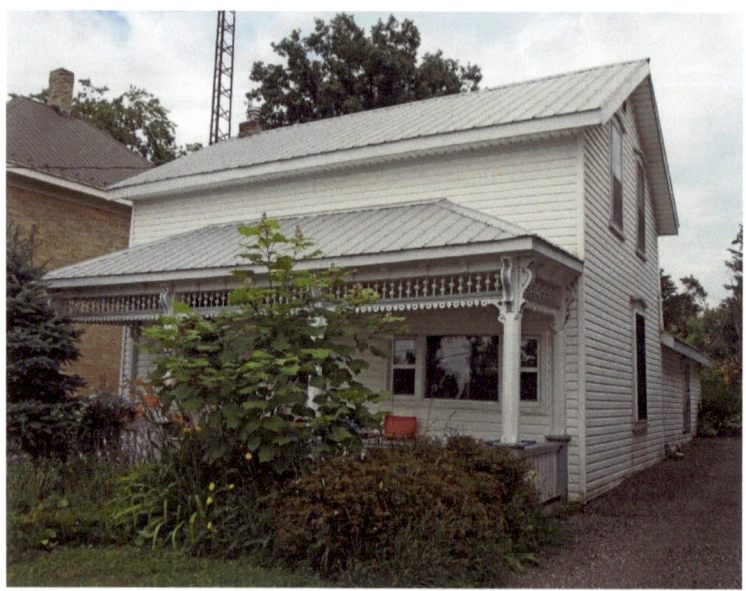

39 Wellington Street

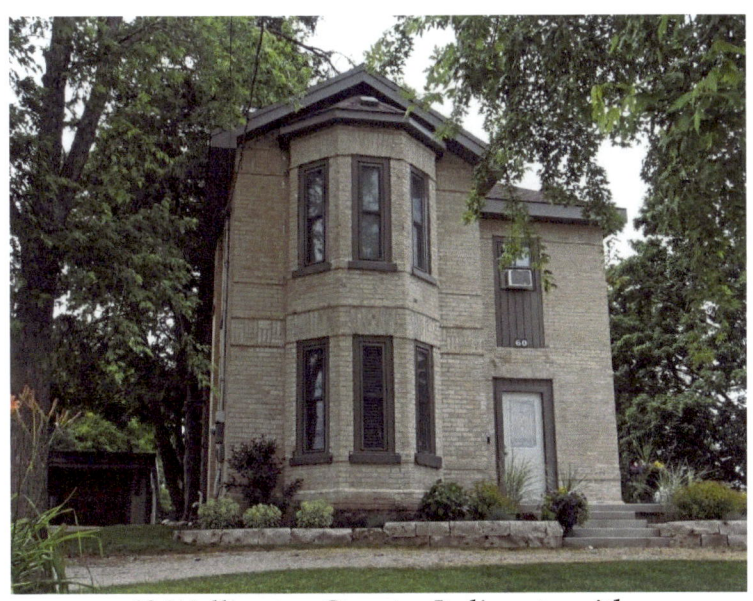

60 Wellington Street – Italianate with
two-storey tower-like bay

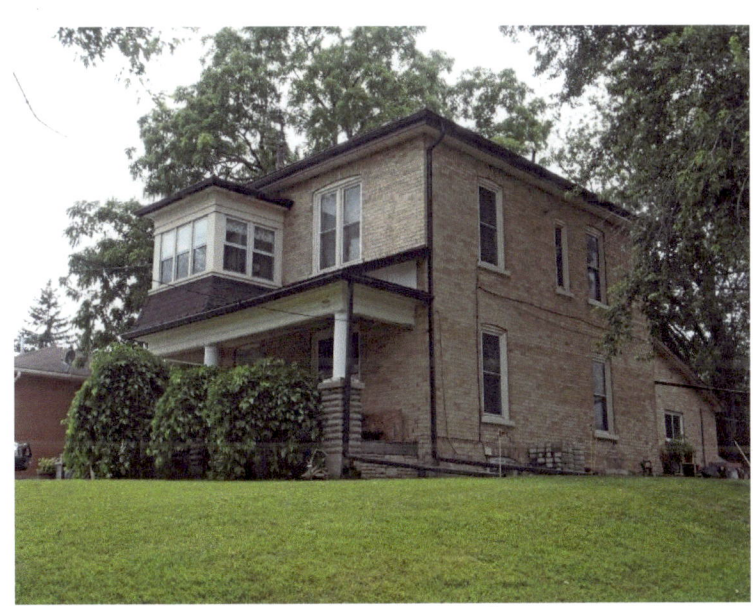

Wellington Street - Italianate

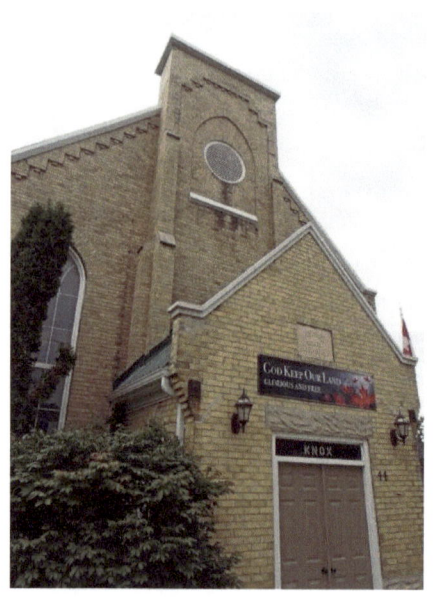

44 Wellington Street – Knox Presbyterian Church c. 1888

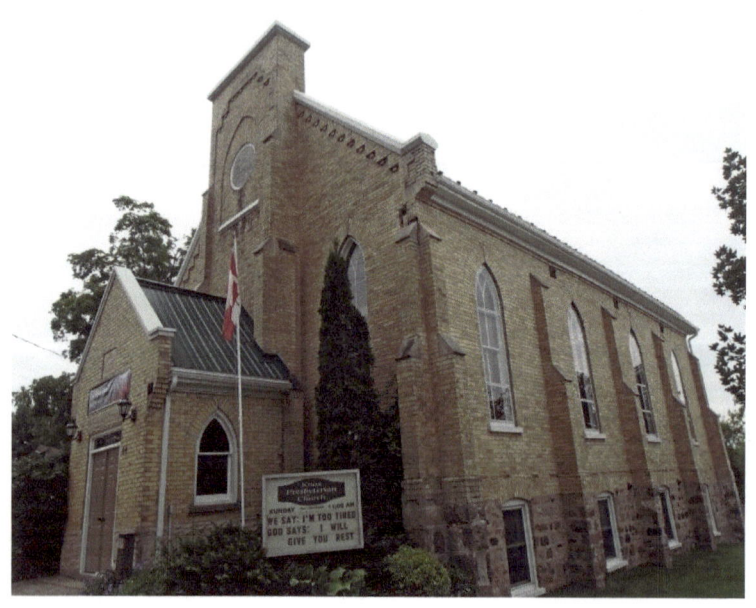

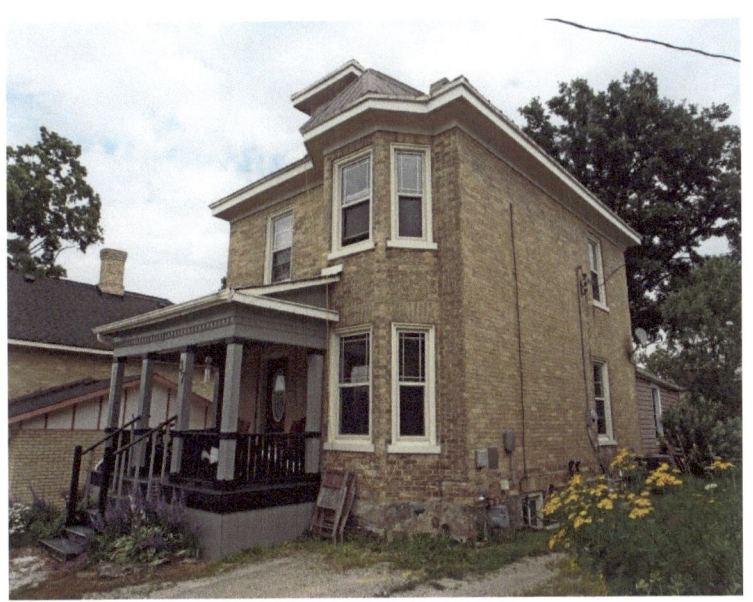

37 Wellington Street – Italianate
with two-storey tower-like bay

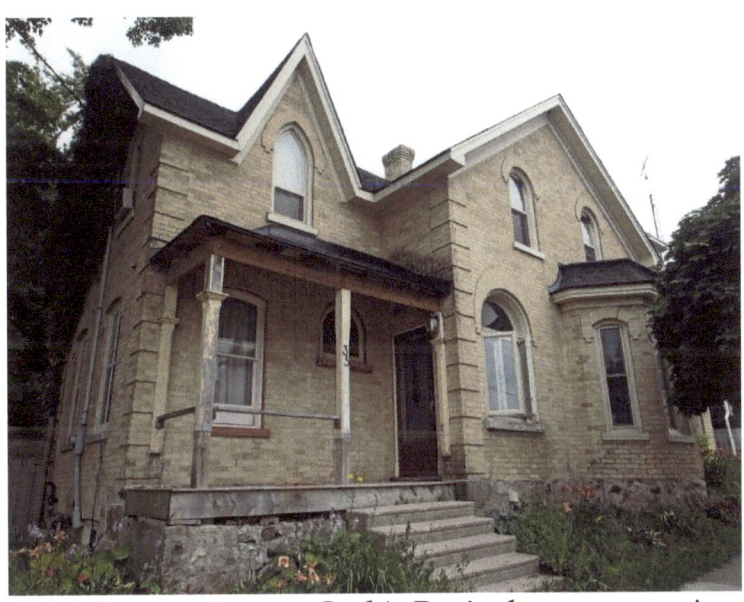

35 Wellington Street – Gothic Revival – corner quoins,
bay window, arched window voussoirs

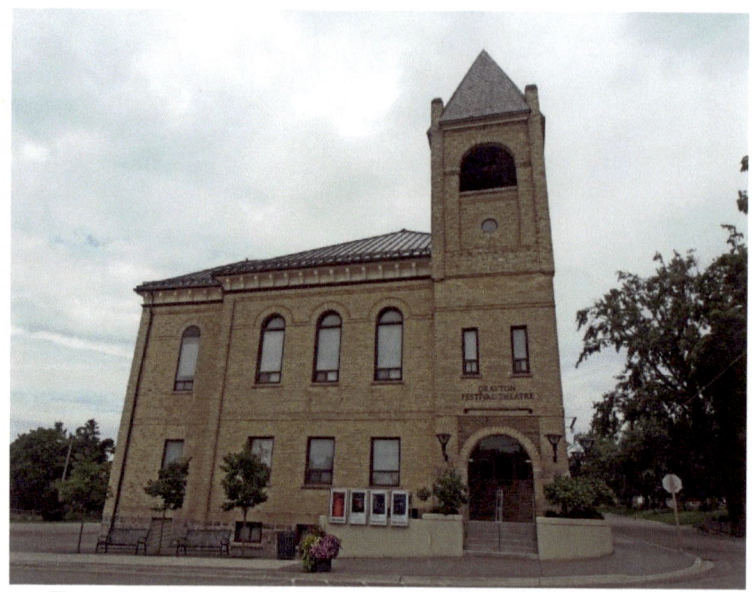

Drayton Town Hall opened 1903 - built to house
Council Chambers, Municipal Offices, library, fire hall,
jail, and opera house

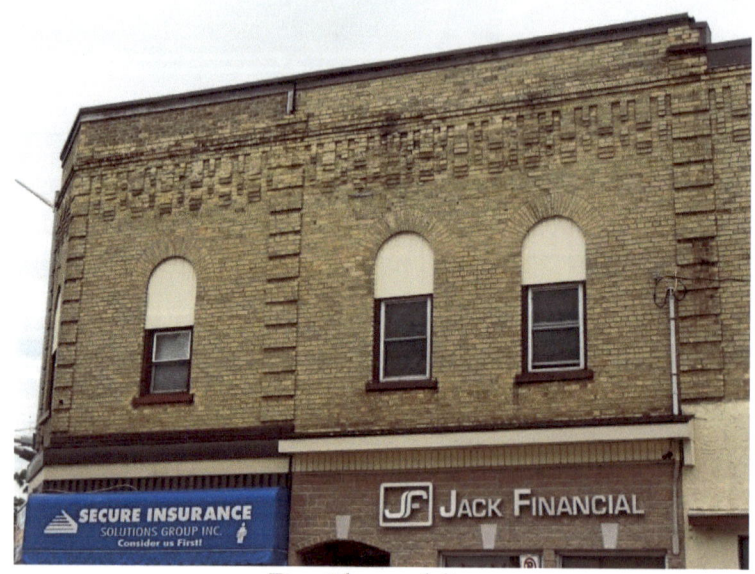

Dentil moulding

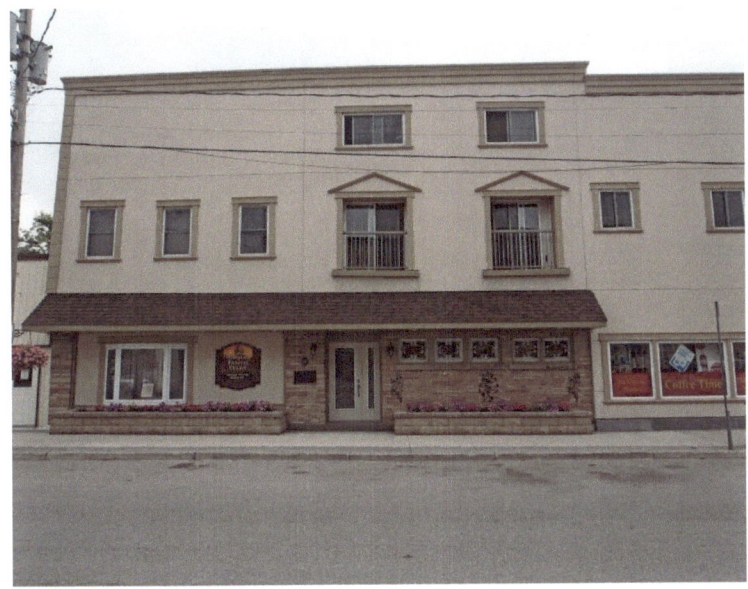

20 Wellington Street South – Drayton Funeral Home – In 1847 Edward Dales established his business as undertaker on this site. It has remained a funeral home to this day.

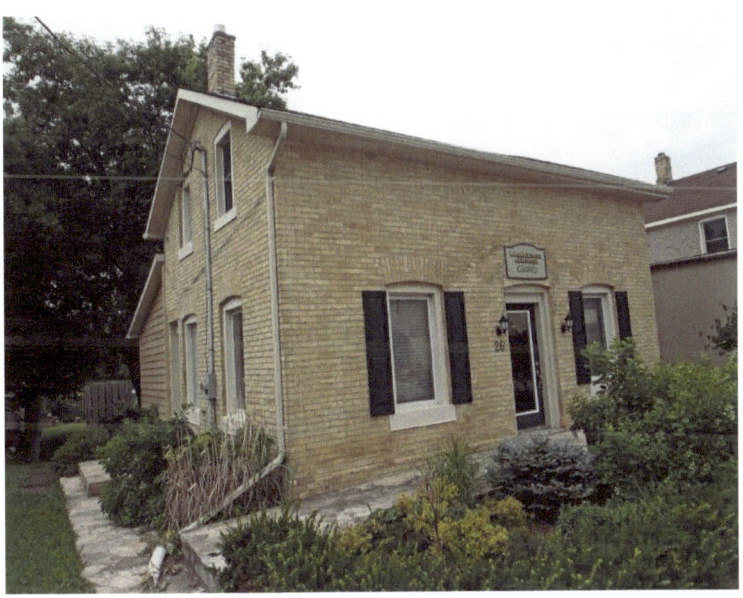

26 Wellington Street

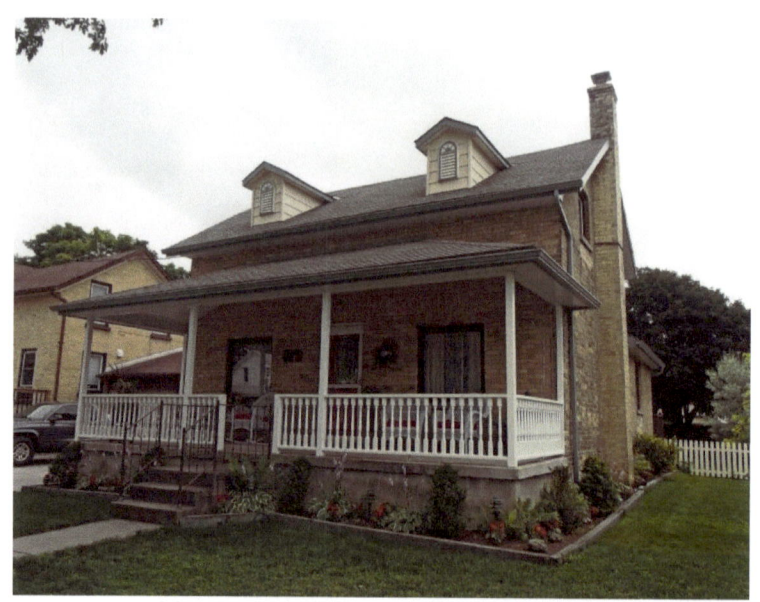

29 Wood Street – dormers in attic

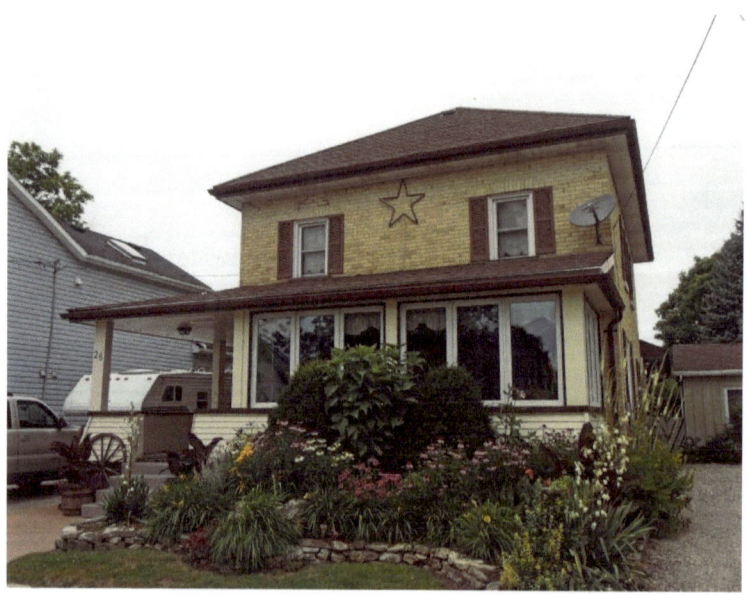

28 Wood Street – hipped roof

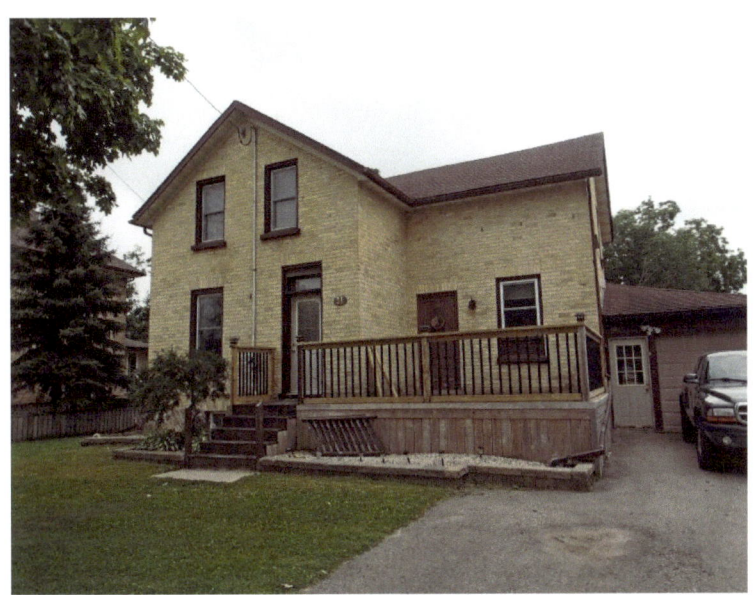

31 Wood Street – Gothic Revival

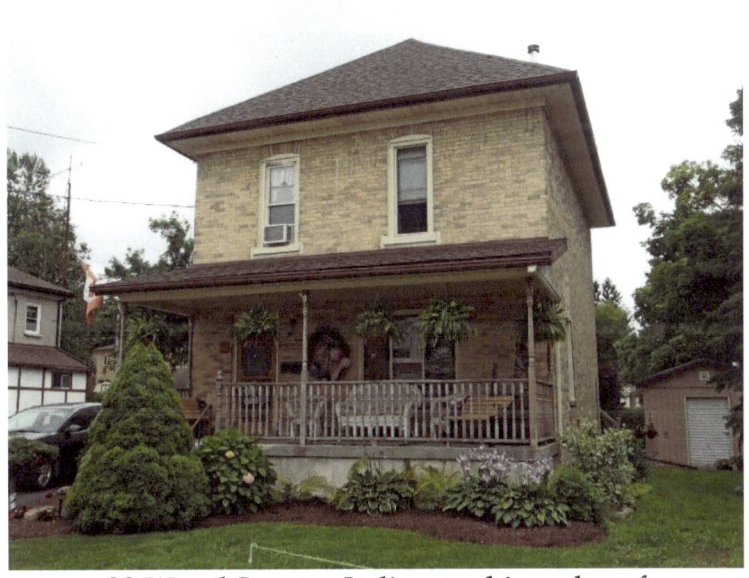

33 Wood Street – Italianate, hipped roof

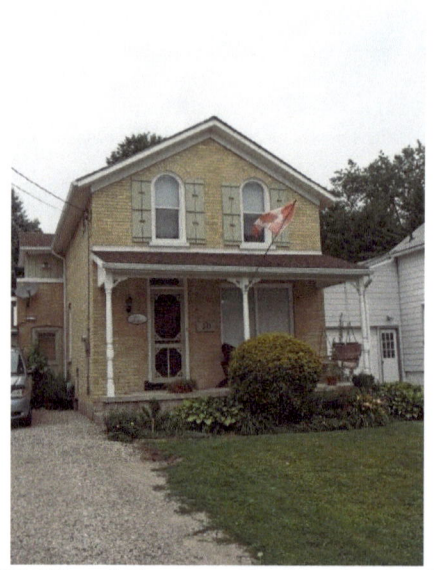

30 Wood Street – Gothic Revival

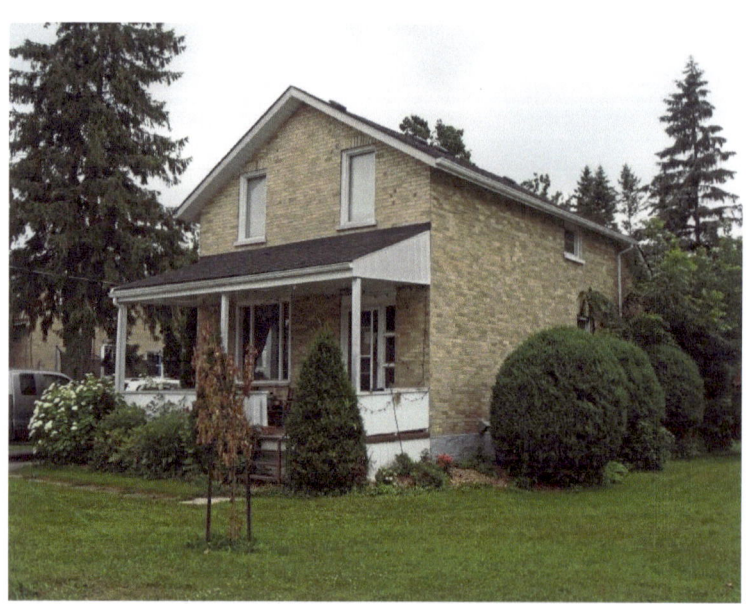

41 Wood Street – Gothic Revival

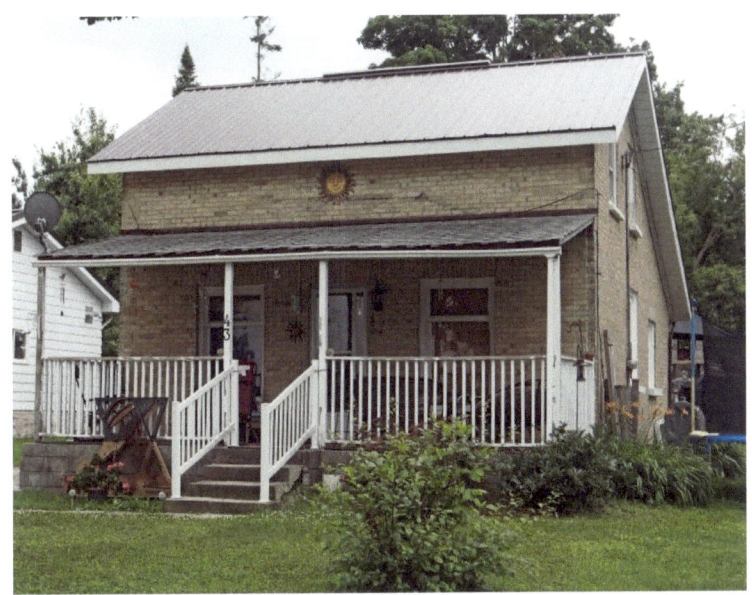

43 Wood Street

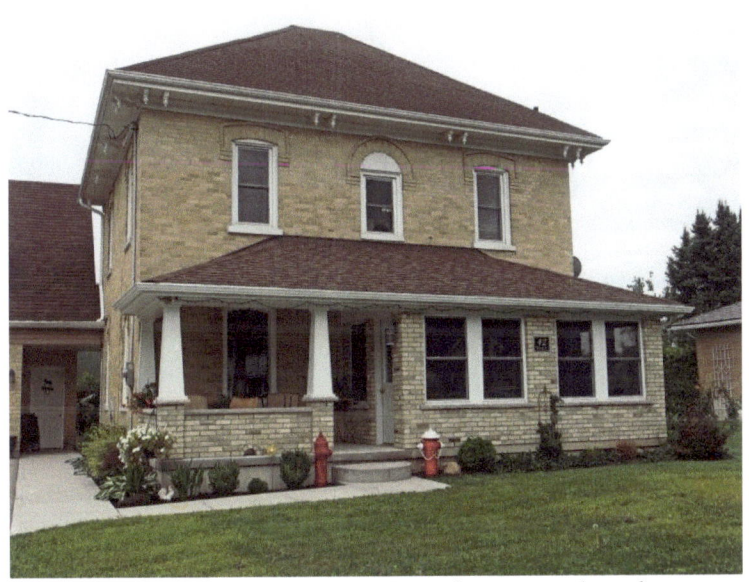

42 Wood Street – hipped roof, cornice brackets

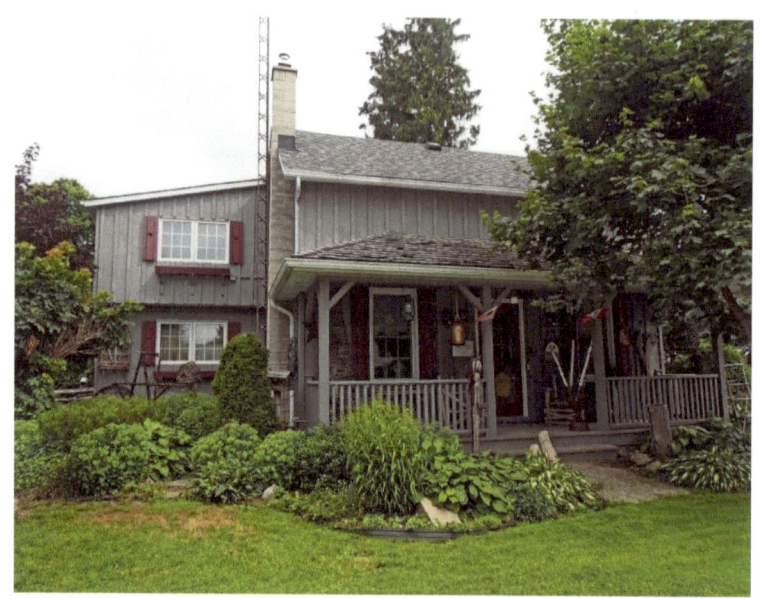

17 John Street

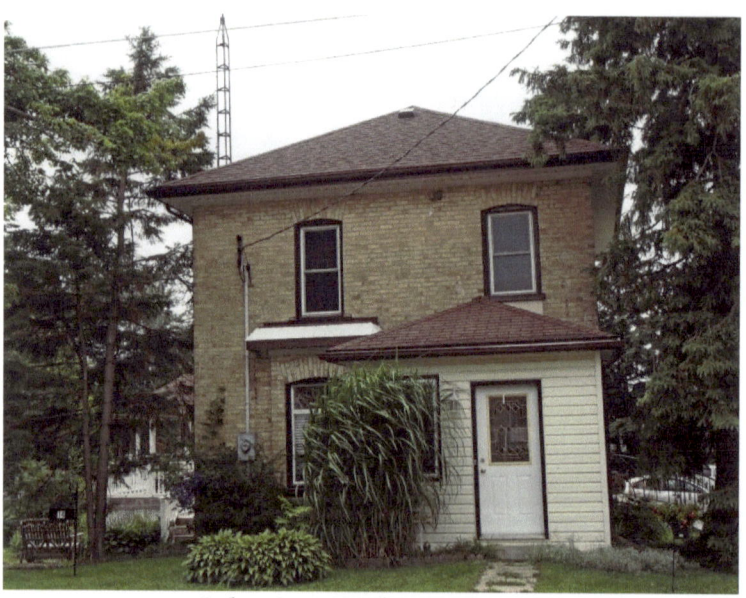

John Street – hipped roof

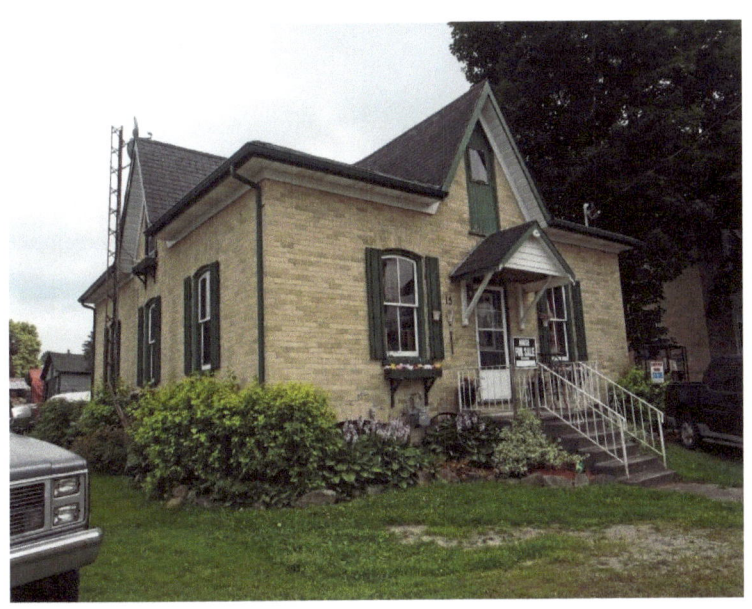

15 John Street – Gothic Revival

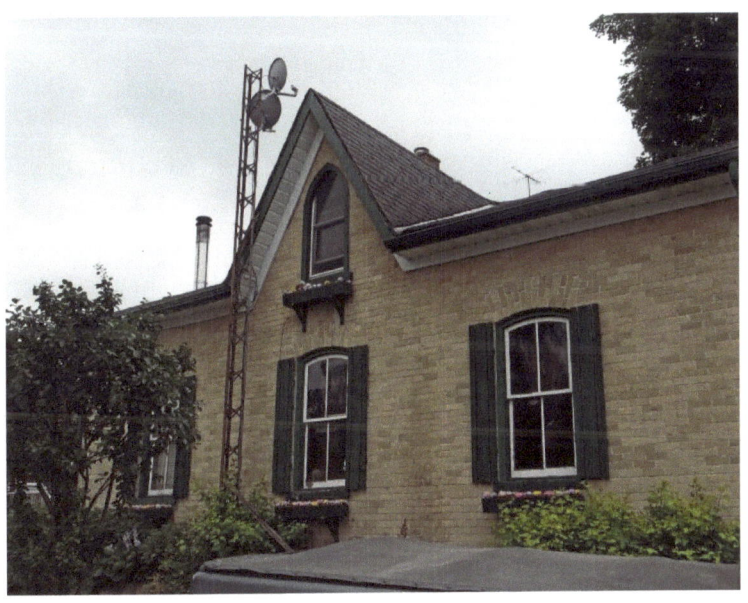

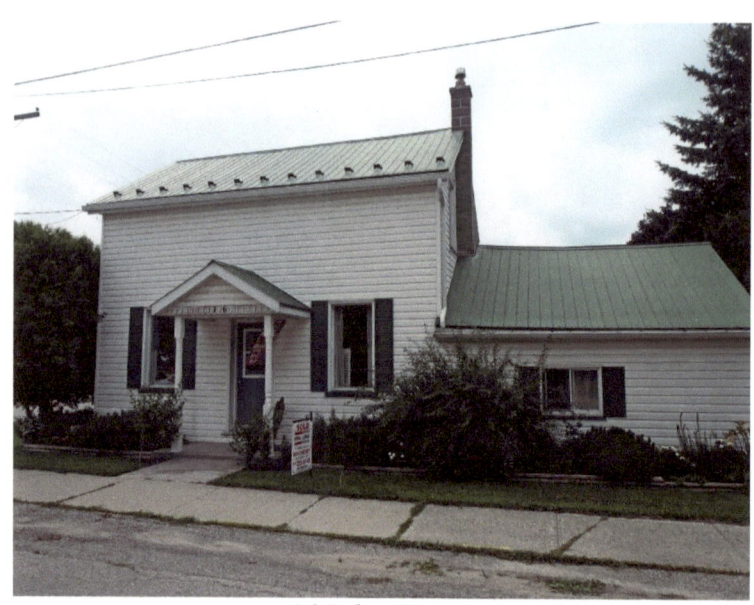

16 John Street

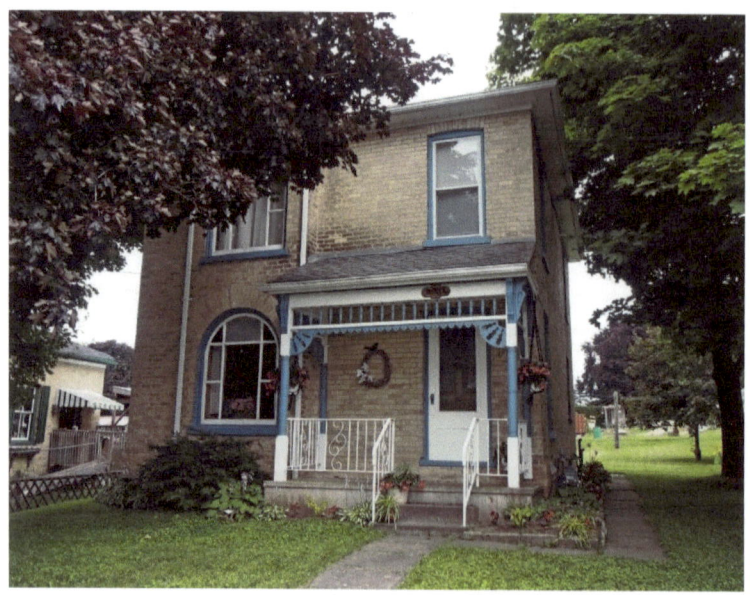

John Street

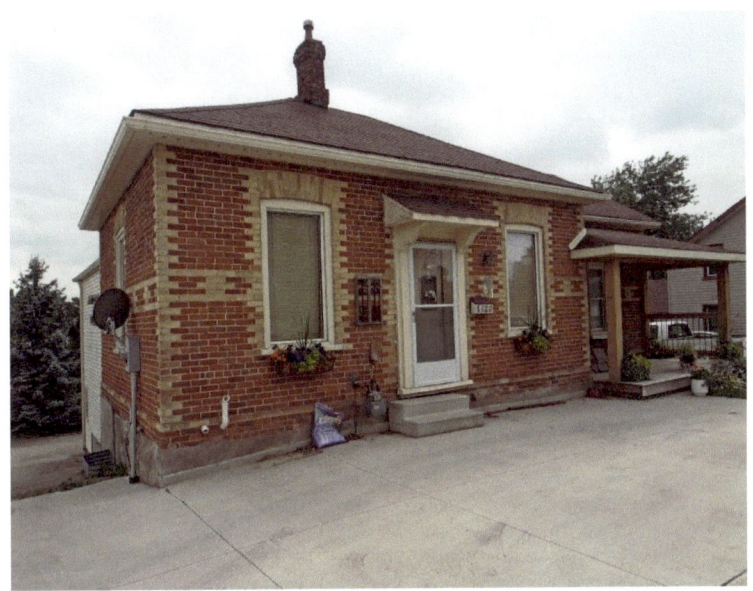

81 John Street – dichromatic brickwork

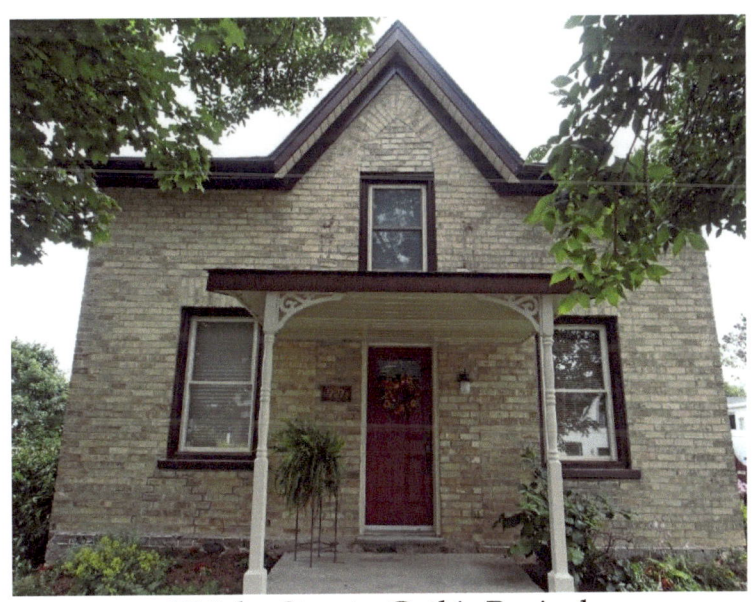

77 John Street – Gothic Revival

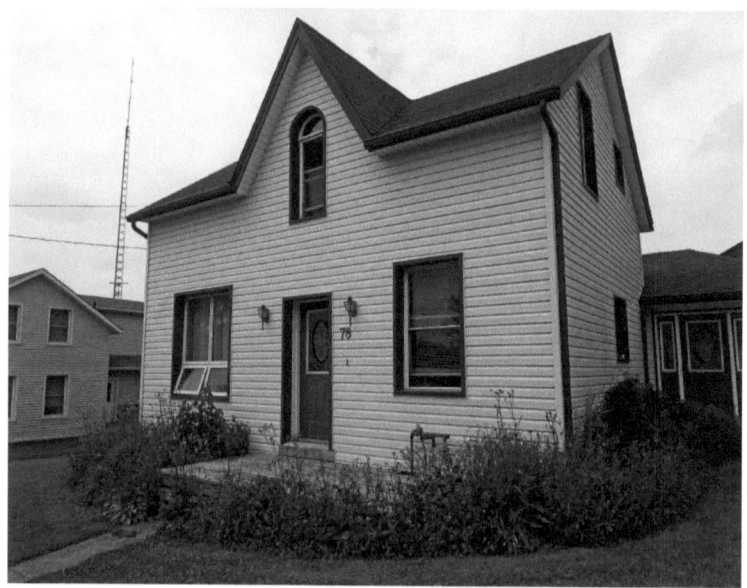

78 John Street – Gothic

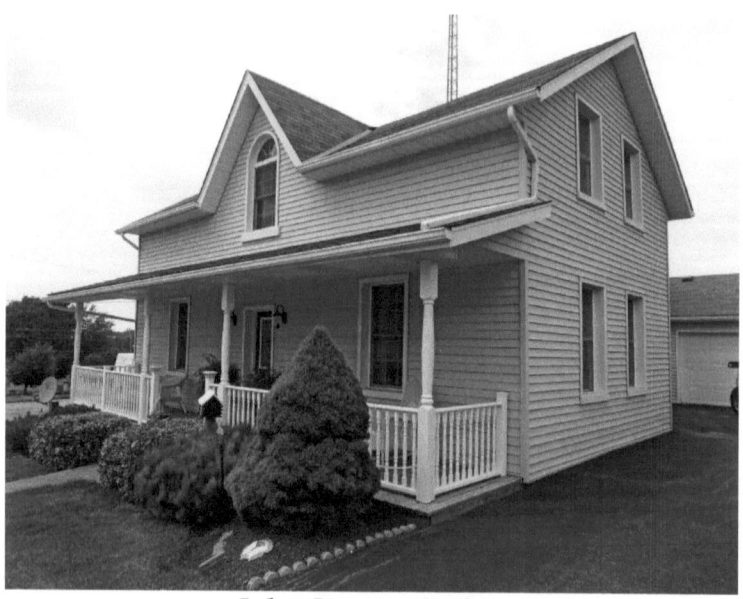

John Street - Gothic

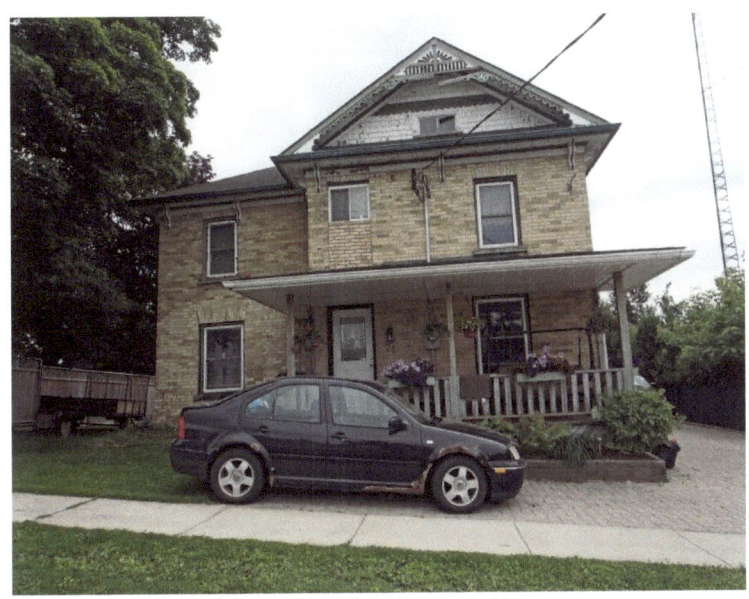

71 John Street

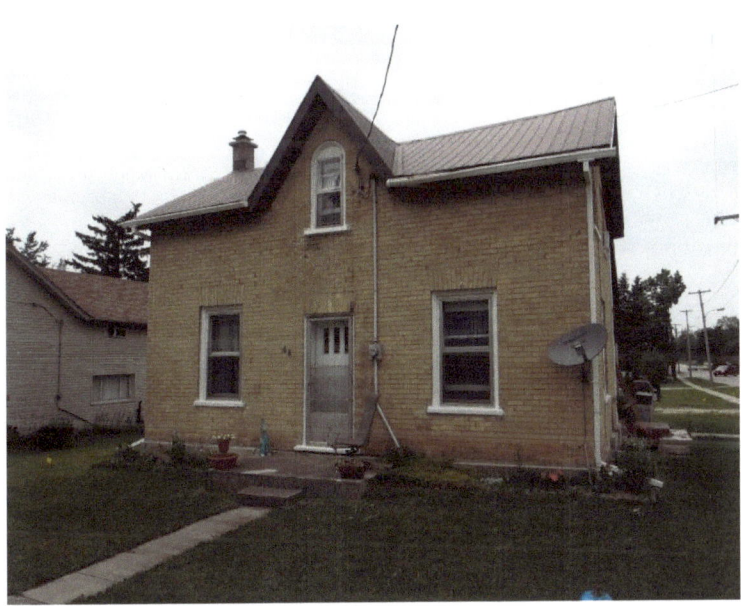

68 Main Street - Gothic

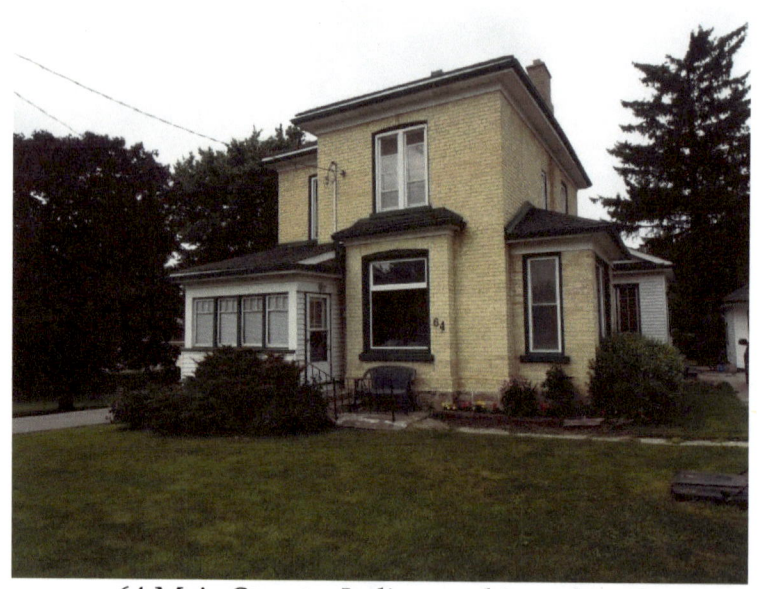

64 Main Street – Italianate, hipped roof

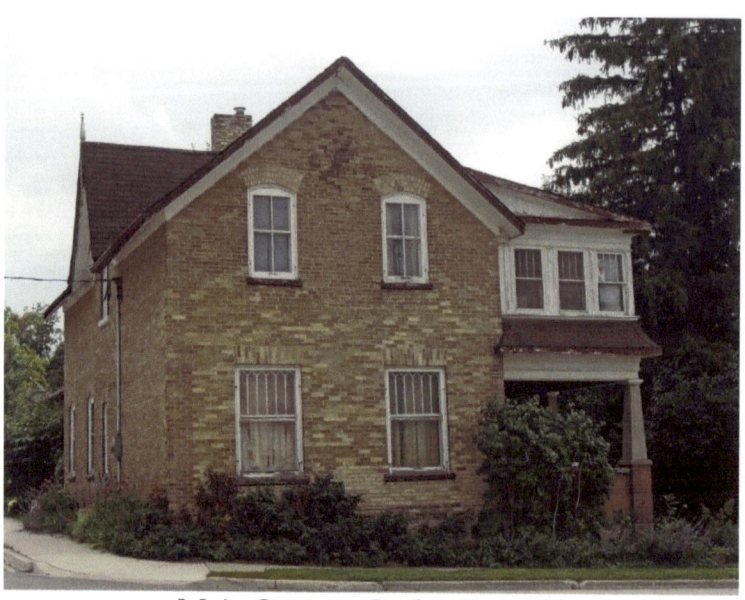

Main Street – Gothic Revival

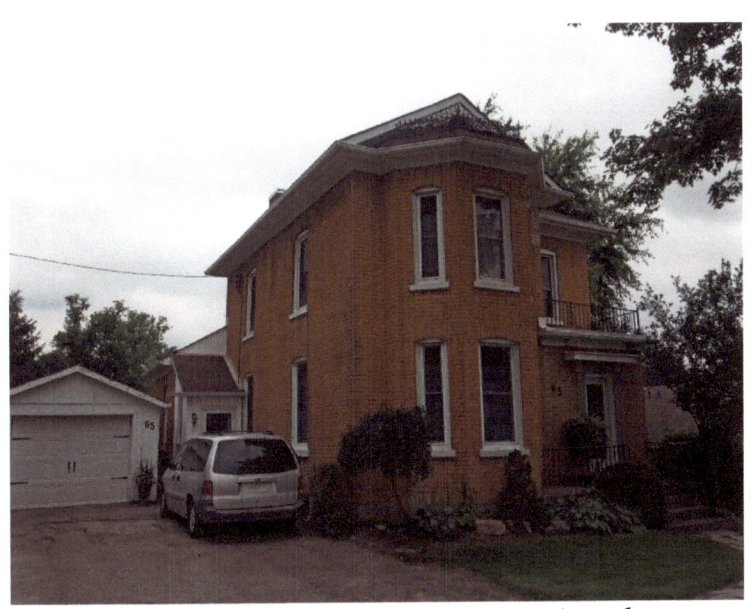

65 Main Street – Italianate, iron cresting above two-storey bay window

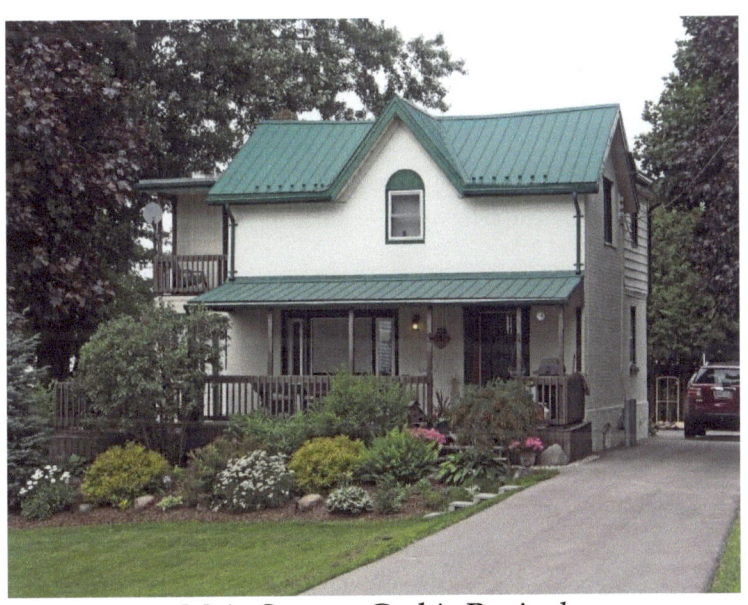

Main Street – Gothic Revival

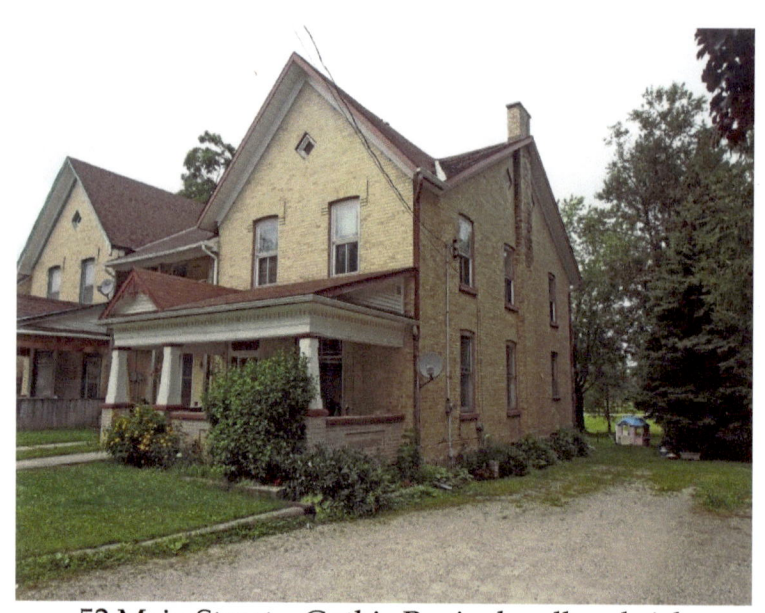

52 Main Street – Gothic Revival, yellow brick

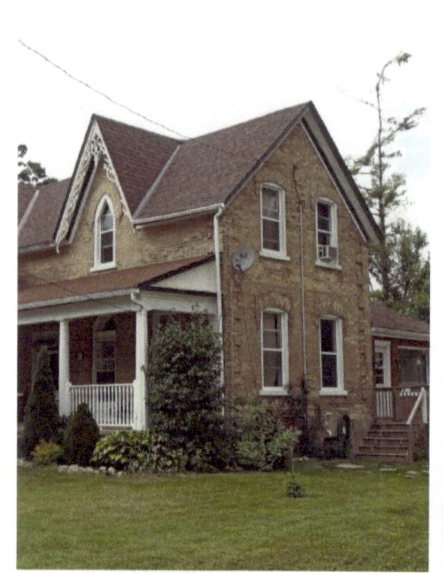

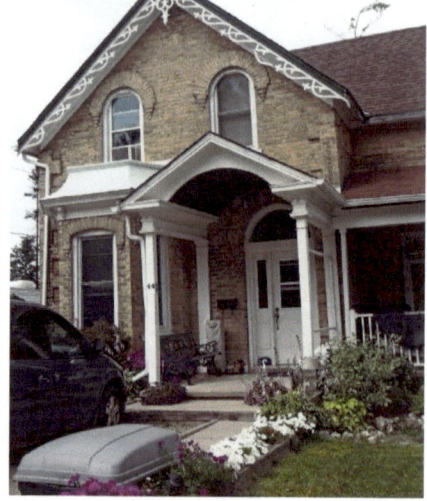

46 Main Street   44 Main Street
Gothic Revival
Vergeboard trim on gables

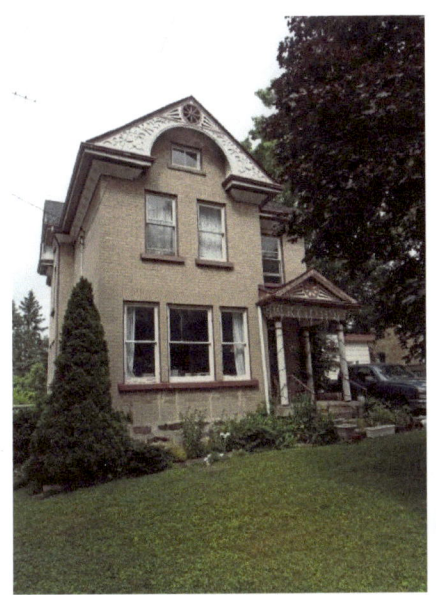

Main Street

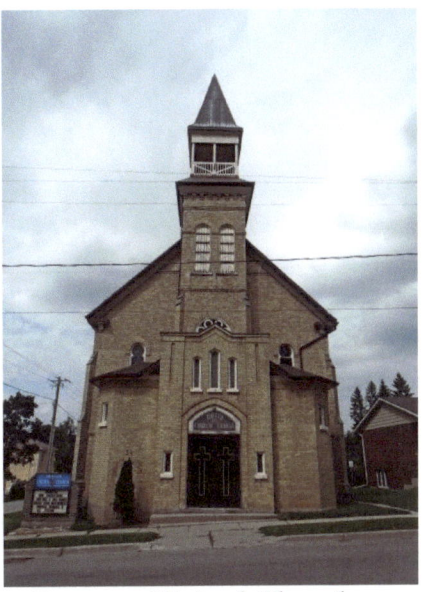

Drayton United Church
A.D. 1892, bell tower,
cobblestone basement

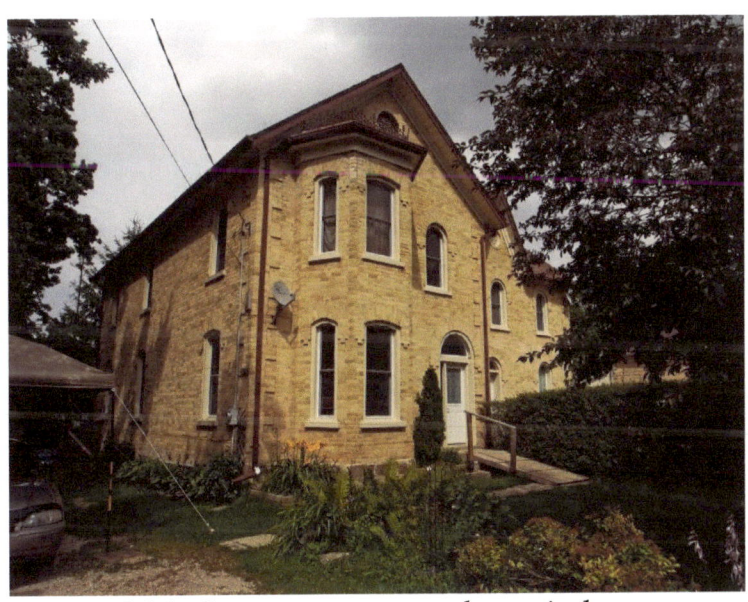

Main Street – two-storey bay window

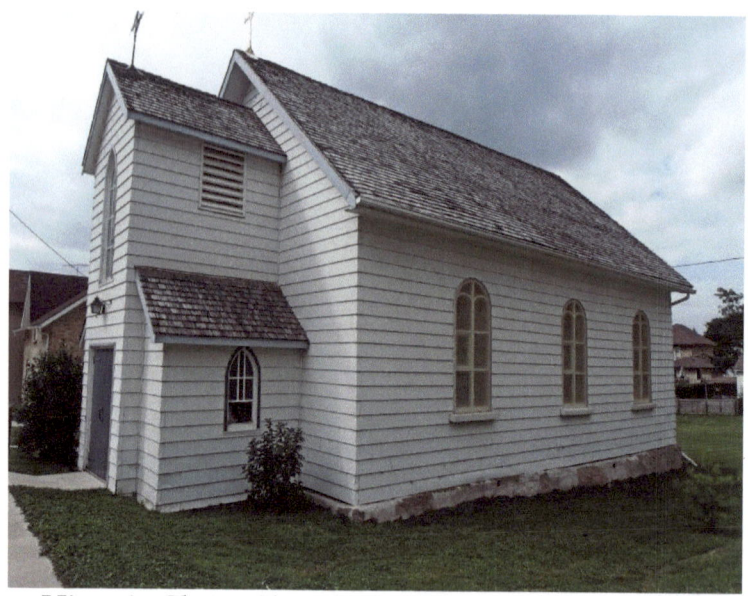

Historic Christ Church Anglican established 1883

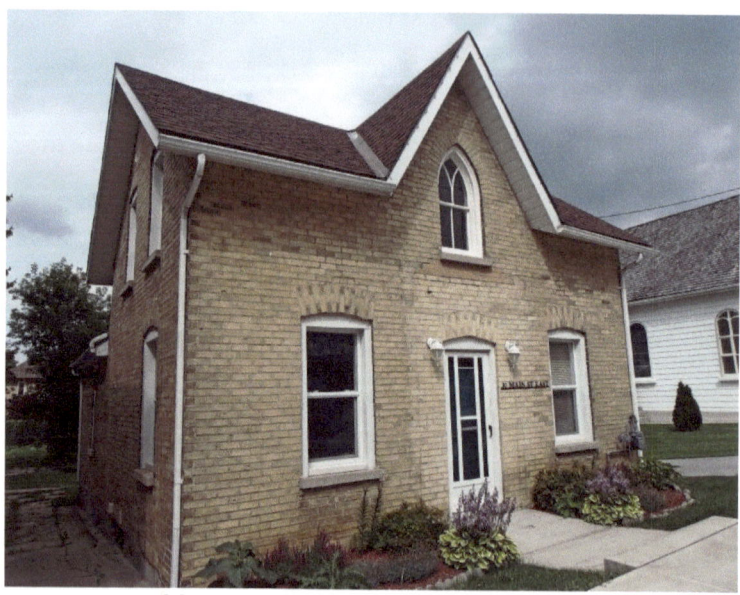

30 Main Street – Gothic Revival

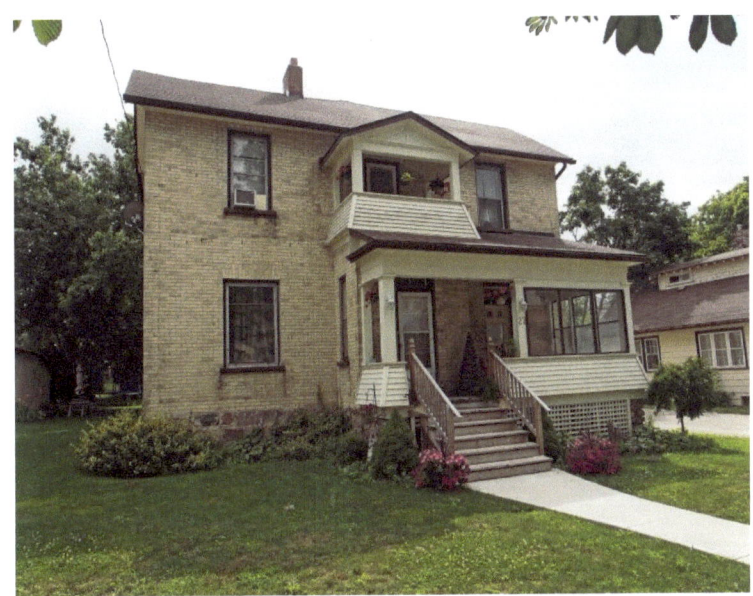

27 Main Street

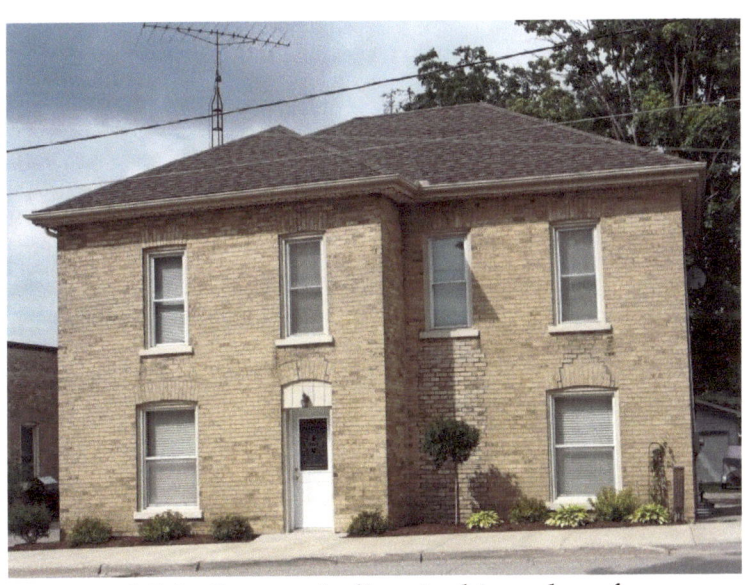

Main Street – Italianate, hipped roof

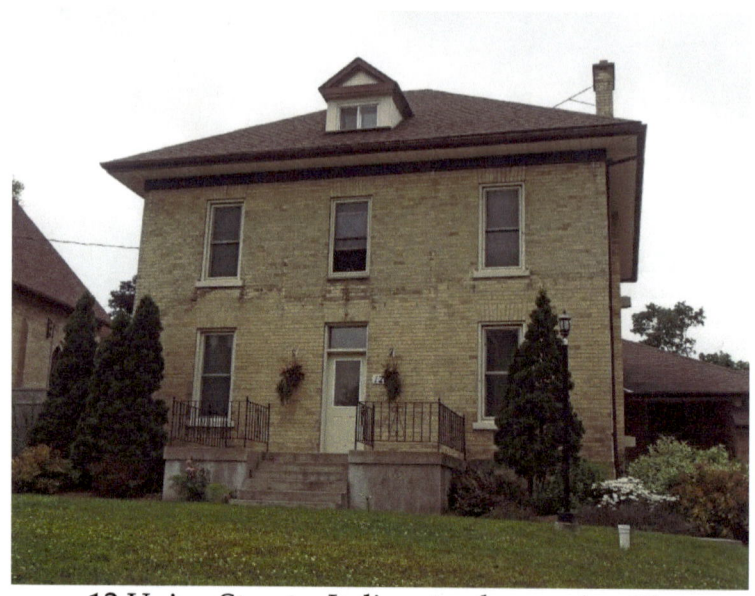

12 Union Street – Italianate, dormer in attic

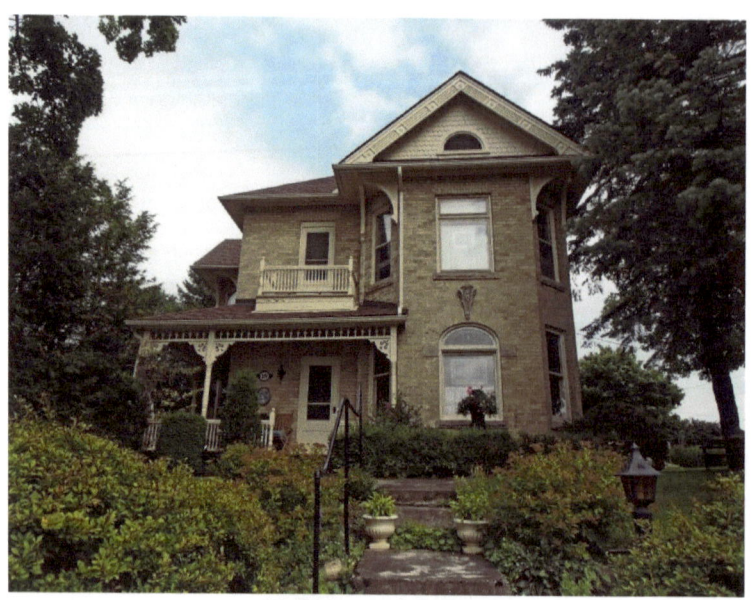

19 Edward Street

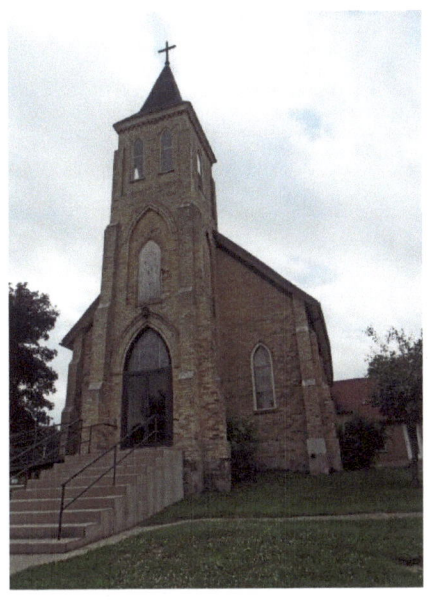

St. Martin of Tours Catholic Church

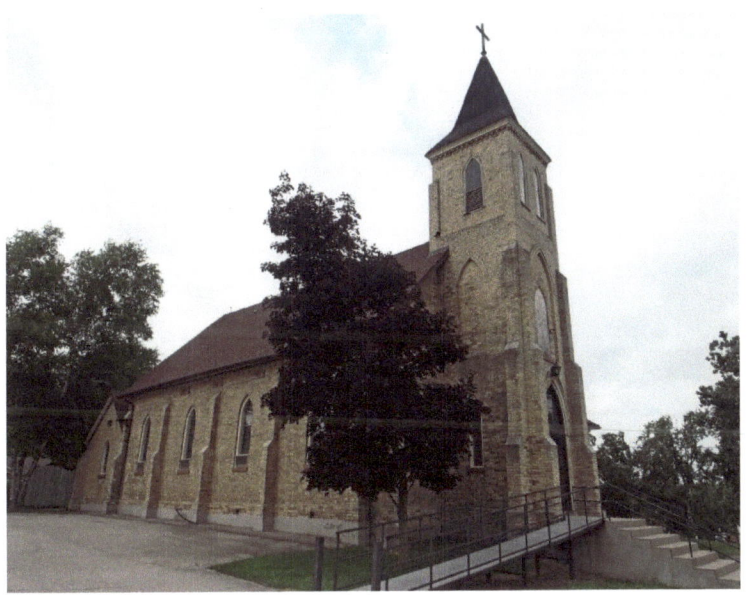

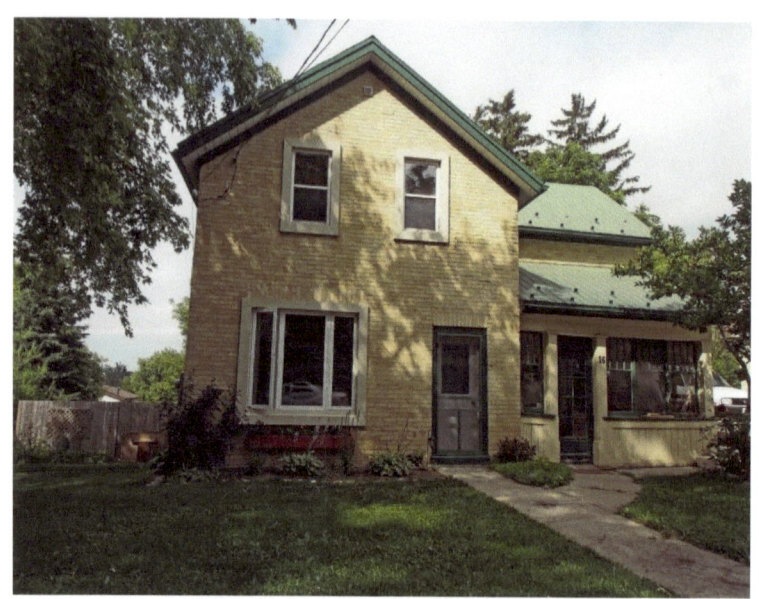

16 High Street – Gothic Revival

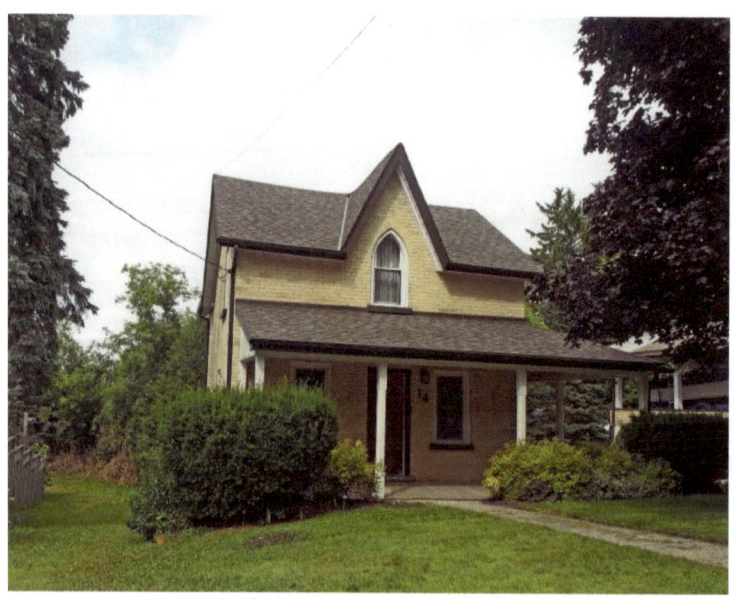

14 High Street – Gothic cottage

Salem

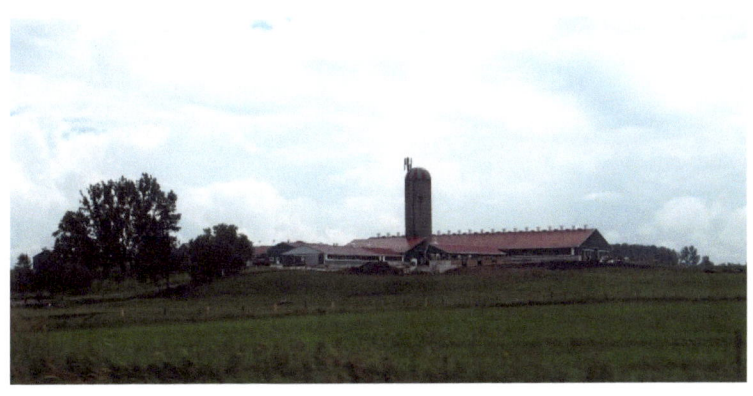

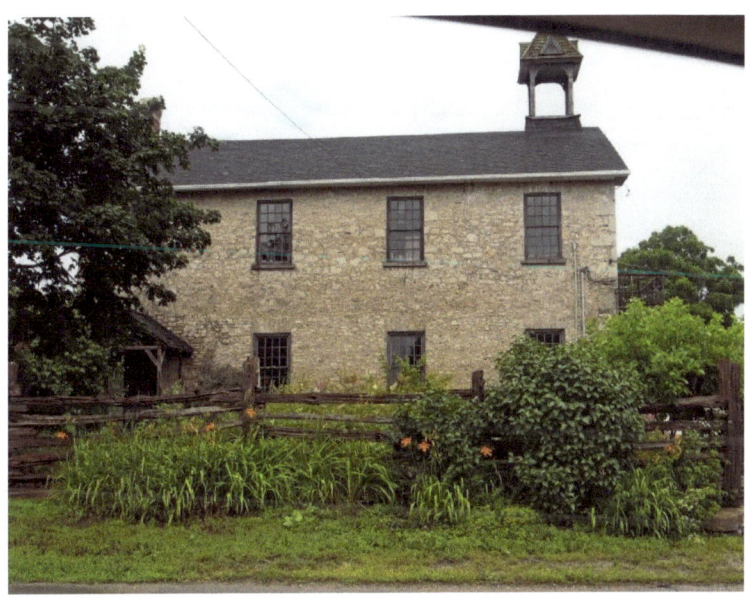

Speedside

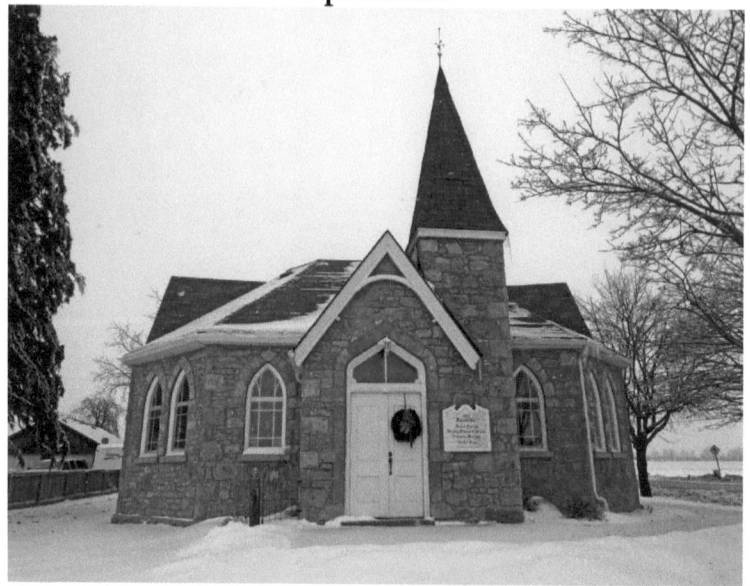

Speedside United Church A.D. 1855

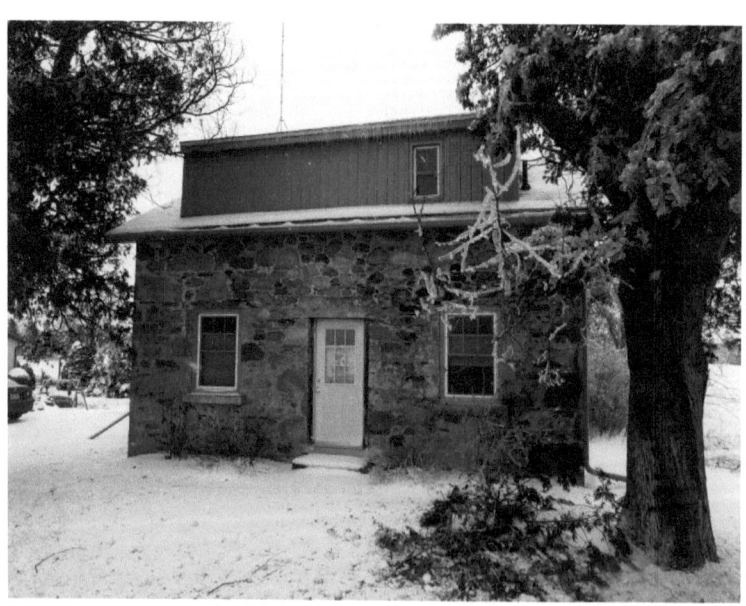

Cobblestone architecture

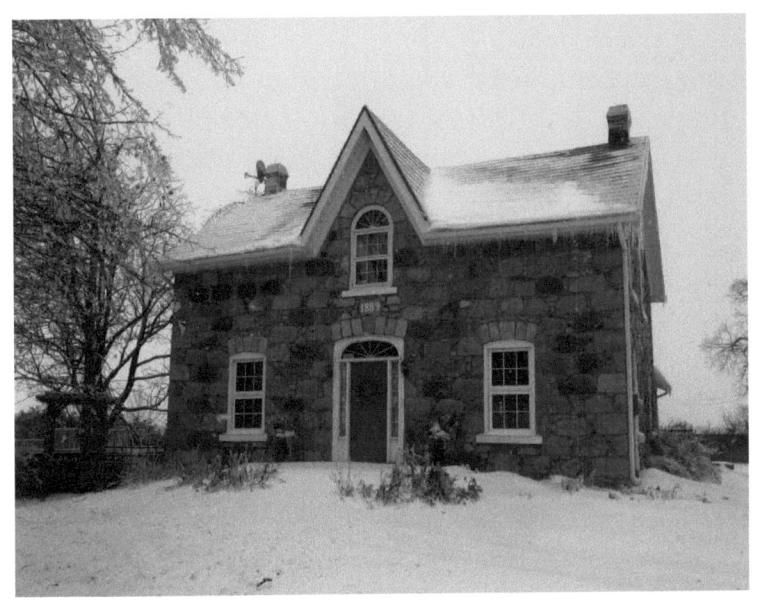

Gothic Revival - cobblestone architecture

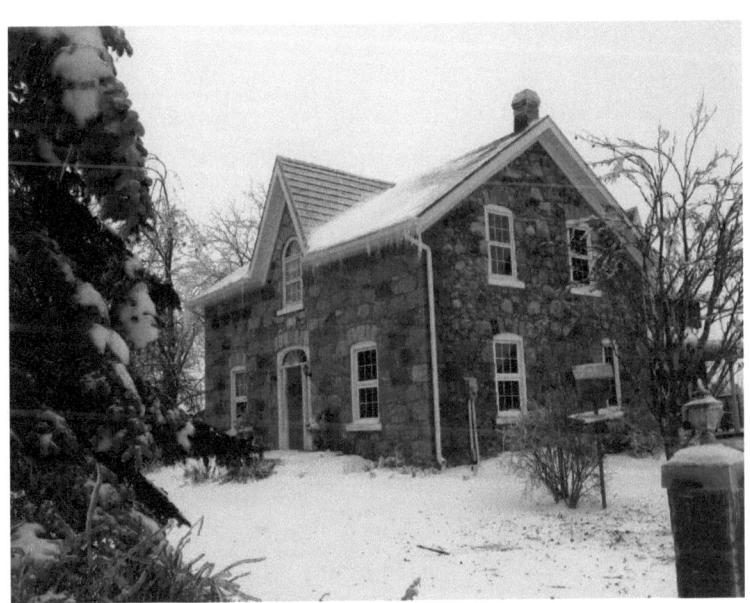

Brackets: a decorative or weight-bearing structural element which forms a right angle with one side against a wall and the other under a projecting surface such as an eave or roof. Example: 24 Main Street, Drayton	
Buttress: a masonry structure built against or projecting from a wall which serves to support or reinforce the wall. In Canadian architecture, they are sometimes used for decoration. Example: Drayton United Church of Canada	
Cobblestone architecture: Refers to the use of cobblestones embedded in mortar as a method for erecting walls on houses and commercial buildings. Example: Drayton United Church	
Dentil Moulding: an even series of rectangles used as ornamental decoration in cornices. Example: Drayton Chop House	
Dichromatic brickwork: the use of two colours of brick, tile or slate to decorate a façade. Example: Alma (see Page 6)	
Dormer: (French for "sleep") a gable end window that pierces through the plane of a sloping roof surface to create usable space in the top floor or attic of a building by adding headroom. Example: 29 Wood Street, Drayton	

Gable: the triangular portion of a wall between the edges of a sloping roof. Example: Alma (see Page 12)	
Hipped Roof: a roof where all sides slope downwards to the walls with no gables. Example: 33 Wood Street, Drayton	
Keystones and Voussoirs: a voussoir is a wedge-shaped element used in building an arch. A keystone is the central stone that locks all the stones into position, allowing the arch to bear weight. A keystone is often enlarged and embellished. Example: Alma (see Page 11)	
Lancet Window: a tall, narrow window with a pointed arch at its top. Example: Drayton United Church	
Quoin: masonry blocks at the corner of a wall, often a decorative feature, usually larger or of a different colour than the rest of the wall. Example: Glen Allan (see Page 19)	
Vergeboard and Finial: also called bargeboards – hang from the projecting end of a roof and are often elaborately carved and ornamented. **Finial:** ornament added to the top of a gable, pinnacle, canopy or spire – a Gothic element. Example: Alma (see Page 6)	

Edwardian, 1900-1930 – This style bridges the ornate and elaborate styles of the Victorian era and the simplified styles of the 20th century. Balanced facades, simple roof lines, dormer windows, large front porches, and smooth brick surfaces are its characteristics. Example: 27 Main Street, Drayton	
Gothic Revival, 1830-1890 – These decorative buildings have sharply-pitched gables with highly detailed vergeboards, pointed-arch window openings, and dichromatic brickwork. It is a common style in Ontario. Example: Alma (see Page 10)	
Italianate, 1850-1900 – It has wide-bracketed eaves, belvederes, wrap-around verandahs. Example: Main Street, Drayton (see Page 30)	
A log cabin, built from logs, was usually one- or 1½-storeys constructed with round rather than hewn, or hand-worked, logs, and erected quickly for frontier shelter. Log cabins were built from logs laid horizontally and interlocked on the ends with notches. Example: Glen Allan (see Page 20)	
Romanesque Revival, 1880-1910 – This style hearkens back to medieval architecture of the 11th and 12th centuries with a heavy appearance, blocky towers and rounded arches. Example: Downtown Drayton (see Page 32)	

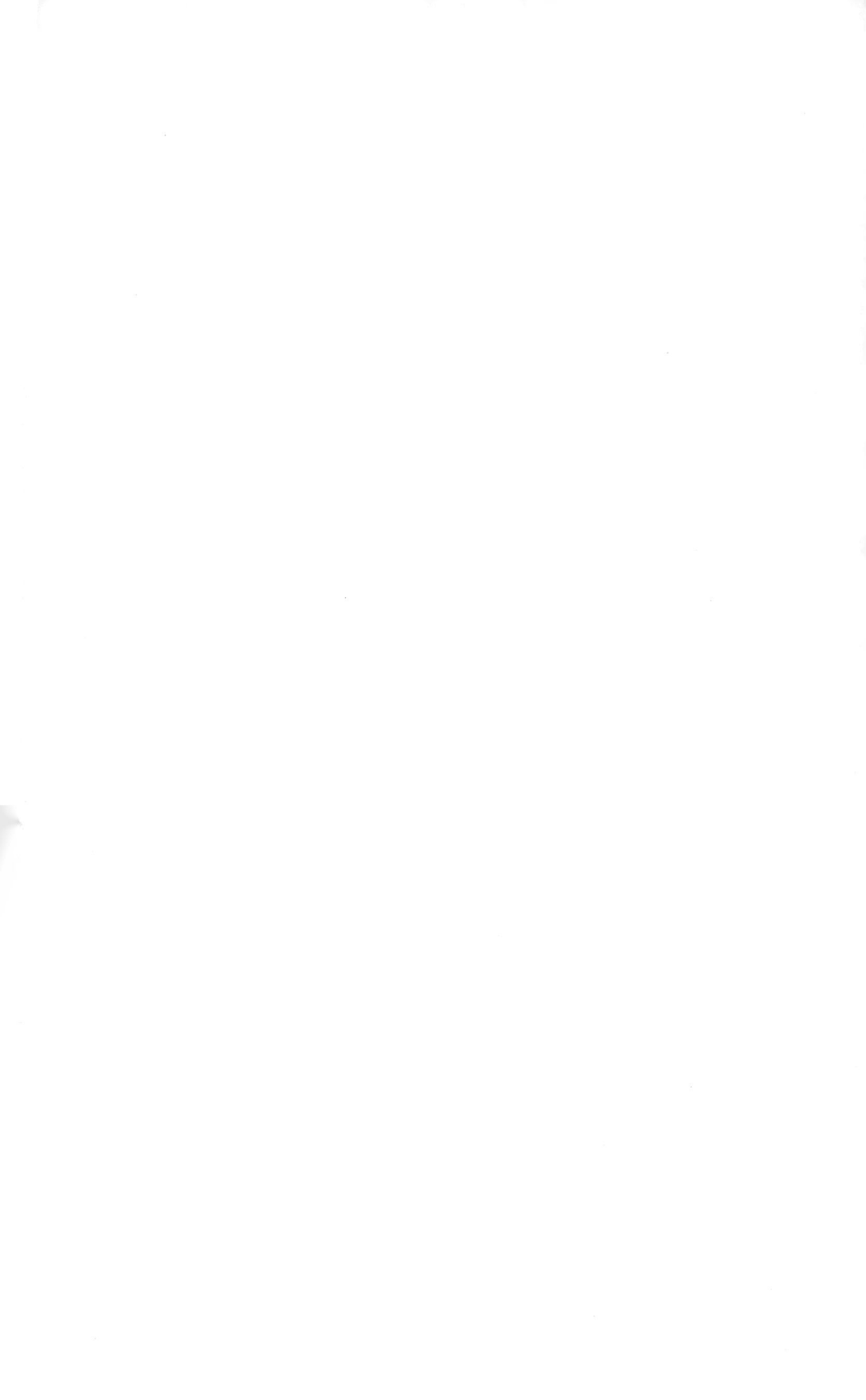